The U.S. Organ Procurement System

AEI EVALUATIVE STUDIES
Marvin H. Kosters
Series Editor

The U.S. Organ Procurement System

A Prescription for Reform

David L. Kaserman
and
A. H. Barnett

The AEI Press

Publisher for the American Enterprise Institute

WASHINGTON, D.C.

2002

Library of Congress Cataloging-in-Publication Data

Kaserman, David L.
    The U.S. organ procurement system: a prescription for reform / David L.
Kaserman and A. H. Barnett.
        p. cm.
    Includes bibliographical references and index.
    ISBN 0-8447-4170-1 (cloth   —ISBN 0-8447-4171-X (pbk.

    1. Procurement of organs, tissues, etc.—United States. 2. Donation of
organs, tissues, etc.—United States. 3. Allocation of organs, tissues, etc.—United
States. 4. Transplantation of organs, tissues, etc.—United States. 5. Procurement
of organs, tissues, etc.—Law and legislation—United States. I. Barnett, A. H.
(Andy Hubbard), 1945– II. Title.

    RD129.5 .K37 2002
    362.1'783'0973—dc21

                                                        2002025402

To those who wait, to those who have died unnecessarily, and to the families of both.

Contents

LIST OF FIGURES

LIST OF TABLES

Foreword

Technology in all areas, but perhaps most especially in biology and medicine, is the hallmark of the modern age. It has made the unimaginable commonplace. Animal species cloning, human gender selection, new and astonishing methods of reproduction, in utero operative procedures, and construction of a genetic "book of life" are but a few of the startling advances. No modern miracle is more welcome or controversial than the technology of organ transplantation. Over a scant four decades, medical techniques and breakthrough pharmaceuticals have greatly improved the success rates of transplants of kidneys, livers, hearts, lungs, and other organs.

Despite the incredible promise of transplants to relieve human suffering, the process has generated enormous controversy. Matters of life and death always elicit strong responses, but organ transplantation has even achieved pulp media immortality over the past decade. From the controversial transplant received by a baseball legend to the sale of kidneys from live "donors" in India, this hot-button issue has generated human interest far beyond the technology or individuals involved. The reason: Current methods of organ procurement have generated acute shortages of cadaveric organs for transplants that create a genuine crisis of "life or death" for many thousands of Americans.

Emotions, lack of information, self-interest, and ignorance on the part of those involved and in society generally rule and mold the debate. Until now, that is. Economists David L. Kaserman and Andy H. Barnett inject sorely needed doses of reason, logic, and good common sense into the transplant dilemma. Isolating the procurement issue from all others (such as organ distribution and ultimate destination), they establish a persuasive and compelling case for markets in cadaveric organs.

The obvious and fundamental problem, as Kaserman and Barnett clearly demonstrate with the tools of Econ 101, is that the quantity of organs demanded exceeds the quantity supplied at an effective zero price of procurement. Waiting lists have consequently grown significantly longer, and deaths of those on these lists have increased dramatically. The system of "express donation" and proscription of an organ procurement market by Congress in 1984 have, in short, been an abject and hideous failure. The authors go on to weigh alternatives and to show how a market system, whereby for-fee arrangements may be made by procurement firms with living donors (for postdeath extraction) or with relatives of deceased potential donors, would work. Using appropriate assumptions, they show that organ prices would likely be well under $1,000 each—adding little to the cost and burden of the transplant recipient (or insurance companies). With preliminary but plausible statistics, moreover, the authors find that a for-fee system would adjust cadaveric organ supplies to demands through time and would save thousands of lives at relatively low cost.

If such widespread benefits would accrue to a market system in organ procurements, why is one not in place? The answer: Some parties flatly and vehemently object to such a system because they claim that market arrangements are "unethical." Such "ethical" arguments and those related to it are fairly and correctly discussed by Kaserman and Barnett and are shown to contain no serious content, particularly when compared with the benefits that could be wrought by a market procurement system. The central question raised by this book, however, remains to haunt society: How many more individuals seeking transplants are going to have to suffer and die in the name of ethics and the status quo?

This well-written and soundly reasoned tract breaks new ground in the analysis and presentation of a most difficult issue. It demonstrates that the depths of misery can be produced in the name of altruism and "ethics." It is a must-read for all medical students, transplant physicians, and the medical community in general. But more. It is a fair, sober, and careful analysis of a problem that so many of us might face on one or the other side of organ transplantation. With the blossoming of new twenty-first–century technologies in this area, ever widening the reach and application of transplantation, it is of far broader interest. In sum, Professors Kaserman and Barnett have produced a book that will serve as a model for how simple economic analysis is able to inform an issue of acute importance to society and, hopefully, increase actual human welfare.

Robert B. Ekelund, Jr.
Lowder Eminent Scholar
Auburn University

Acknowledgments

This monograph pulls together, updates, and extends a continuing line of research that its authors, along with several colleagues, have pursued over the past decade or so. As a result, the analysis presented here has benefited greatly from the input of our coauthors on the published works that have preceded this effort. Specifically, A. Frank Adams, T. Randolph Beard, and Roger D. Blair have all contributed significantly to the earlier work on which this study is based. We are very grateful for their help. In addition, our colleague, Robert B. Ekelund, Jr., generously provided suggestions early on in the formation of this project and wrote the foreword that accompanies it. Ann Rayburn of the Alabama Organ Bank helped us grapple with the rather complex system of interrelated institutions that currently implement U.S. organ procurement policies. We appreciate her help as well.

This work has also benefited substantially from the thoughtful and constructive comments provided by participants in a workshop sponsored by the American Enterprise Institute that focused on an earlier version of this monograph. The following people were kind enough to read the manuscript and offer a number of suggestions, virtually all of which we incorporated in the final version: Jayanta Bhattacharya, Carolyn Colladay, Thomas W. Hazlett, John Hoff, Jimmy Light, Sam Peltzman, Thomas G. Peters, Cindy Spears, and Martin Zelder. While not all of these individuals may agree with all of our opinions, they did appear to agree that the overriding concern of any policy change should be patients' welfare. We offer our sincere appreciation for the efforts of those commentators.

Finally, we owe a special debt of gratitude to Robert B. Helms and Marvin H. Kosters of the American Enterprise Institute. Without their help, we could not have completed this project.

The U.S. Organ Procurement System

1

Introduction

The current system is the problem and it will not be rehabilitated by
further tinkering; a new system is needed.
                                        —David E. Jeffries[1]

The first successful human organ transplant in the United States was performed on December 23, 1954. On that date, a kidney was transplanted
from a living donor who was an identical twin of the recipient. Since then,
organ transplantation technology has improved enormously, with the
principal source of that improvement being the discovery of new immunosuppressive drugs and the increased knowledge of how to use them to prevent organ rejection more effectively. Among the more important discoveries
has been the drug cyclosporine, which was approved for commercial use in
the United States in 1983. Subsequently, as this drug has become more
widely prescribed, as new immunosuppressants have been discovered, as
experience has been gained in administering them, and as surgical techniques have advanced, transplant success rates have improved dramatically.
Today, one-year patient survival rates have reached between 76 and 94
percent for heart, liver, pancreas, and kidney transplant recipients.[2]

Because the primary cause of transplant failure is rejection, the strides
made in immunosuppressive therapy have led to greatly expanded use of
this treatment modality. The two most fundamental advancements have
been the use of organs from recently deceased individuals (as opposed to
living donors), and, because of the ability to use cadaveric organs, transplantation of vital organs other than kidneys (for example, hearts, livers, and
lungs). As a result of those advancements, organ transplantation has now
emerged as an important form of treatment for a variety of life-threatening
diseases. Today, kidneys, hearts, livers, lungs, pancreases, and other organs

are transplanted regularly both to relieve suffering and to prolong life. In 1999 almost 22,000 transplants were performed.[3]

Moreover, unlike many new medical technologies that tend to prolong a patient's life without significantly improving the quality of that life, organ transplantation often restores the patient's health to a level approximating that experienced before the onset of the disease. A successful transplant can provide a patient with a feeling of virtual rebirth and allow a return to a full and productive life. In that regard, organ transplantation stands out as one of the most significant medical advances of the past few decades.

As has occasionally occurred with other such advances, however, the technological success of organ transplantation has spawned a public policy dilemma. Specifically, under existing organ procurement policies, rising success rates and other factors have caused the quantity of cadaveric organs demanded for transplantation to exceed by far the number supplied each year. The resulting annual shortages, in turn, have created a large, growing backlog of patients who are placed on official waiting lists for needed organs. Today, those lists contain over 67,000 patients.[4] The chronic shortage and mounting backlog of desperate patients have sparked heated debate about how best to manage and, more importantly, resolve the persistent undersupply of transplantable organs. Despite this ongoing debate, however, the shortage remains; and the failure of public policy to resolve it has prevented full realization of the potential social benefits of transplantation technology.

Two recent events have heightened public awareness of the shortage of cadaveric organs. First, in 1996 former baseball star Mickey Mantle received a liver transplant within a relatively brief period of time after being placed on the organ recipient waiting list. Cries of favoritism followed, and the transplant community was accused of violating the standard protocol applied to organ allocation decisions. Mr. Mantle's need for and comparatively rapid receipt of a liver transplant had the desirable effect of bringing widespread attention to the plight of thousands of other sufferers of heart, liver, lung, and kidney failure whose lives depend on timely receipt of a suitable organ for transplantation. At the same time, however, it also brought considerable suspicion and outright scorn regarding the fundamental integrity of the current system used to allocate those scarce organs.[5] Such negative attitudes, in turn, may have adverse effects on the willingness of some individuals to donate organs.[6]

More recently, in 1998 the U.S. Department of Health and Human Services proposed major revisions in the system used to allocate organs among potential transplant recipients.[7] Specifically, under the proposed rules, the health status of individual patients (that is, the medical "need" for the transplant operation) would assume increased importance in determining which patients would receive a given organ. The patient's location within the organ procurement organization's franchised collection region would become correspondingly less important under the revised system. The effect of those new rules would be to erode—if not eliminate—the already limited de facto property rights transplant centers have in the organs collected within their respective geographic regions.[8] The fear on the part of many is that, if implemented, the rules would reduce organ collection rates still further as the relatively successful procurement regions are forced to ship many of the organs they collect to the less successful regions. As a result, even fewer organs could become available under the revised system.[9]

Both events have had the beneficial effect of increasing public awareness of the organ shortage and the associated suffering it causes. At the same time, however, they have had the undesirable effect of focusing attention on issues related to the fairness of organ *allocation* rather than the efficiency of organ *collection*. Although allocation problems certainly are important under shortage conditions, they should not divert attention away from the more crucial issue of how to eliminate the underlying cause of such problems—the shortage itself. If the organ shortage can be resolved, allocation issues will become moot.

Over the years, a series of legislative and regulatory actions have been adopted to encourage increased organ donation and, hopefully, thereby to alleviate the shortage.[10] To date, however, all the policy initiatives implemented both in the United States and abroad share one common predominant feature—all have failed to eliminate the shortage of cadaveric organs made available for transplantation. This glaring and longstanding failure has not gone unnoticed. Several commentators have noted the demonstrated inability of current procurement policies to correct the problem they are ostensibly intended to address. For example, Jeffries writes:

> Although the United States system of organ procurement has gone through several modifications, all changes and "improvements" share one thing in common: they all failed to increase the supply of organs. . . . Many countries have tried these systems of increasing organ supply as well as other systems not yet discussed. Unfortunately, none have shown any significant ability to solve the shortage.[11]

Importantly, the failure of existing policies to eliminate the shortage is not attributable to an inadequate number of organs available for transplantation. Of the 2 million or so deaths that occur in the United States each year, estimates indicate that somewhere between 13,000 and 29,000 occur under circumstances that would allow the organs of the deceased to be transplanted.[12] Of those, only 5,843 (or 28 percent of the middle of the range of prior estimates) yielded organ donations in 1999, which was only forty-one more donors than the preceding year.[13] Given the likely number of potential cadaveric organ donors, a more effective procurement policy could, in principle, increase collections by two- or even threefold. Thus, the organ shortage is the product of a failed public policy, not of nature.[14]

Because of the growing shortage and increasing recognition that the problem will not be solved under the present system of procurement, the time now appears ripe for a comprehensive evaluation of alternative cadaveric organ procurement policies. Several considerations suggest the timeliness of such a fundamental reevaluation. First, within the past decade, the shortage situation has grown progressively worse, and the harms it is inflicting have become increasingly intolerable. Expected waiting times for potential transplant recipients that were once measured in months are now stretching into years, and the death toll directly attributable to the shortage is mounting apace.[15] Second, it appears that the political support for continued maintenance of the current system is beginning to erode somewhat as transplant physicians become increasingly frustrated at watching their patients die unnecessarily because of the lack of a suitable cadaveric donor organ. Historically, the most stringent and politically effective opposition to consideration of alternative organ procurement policies—particularly those that rely upon any sort of market mechanism—has come from the medical community.[16] While medical professional organizations continue to champion the current system and oppose any fundamental policy change, individual physicians appear to be increasingly willing to consider alternative approaches.[17] And third, a considerable, though highly diffuse, volume of literature has developed over the past decade or so that explores various alternative policy approaches to resolving the organ shortage. That literature provides valuable information that may be applied to a broad-ranging policy evaluation. Thus, some hope exists that policymakers may finally address this problem in an open, logical, and systematic fashion. That hope, in turn, provides the motivation for this monograph.

To facilitate our discussion, we have chosen to limit the focus of our inquiry in several respects. First, we limit our attention primarily to organ procurement rather than to organ *allocation* policy. In our view, procurement is, by far, the more crucial issue. Inadequate procurement—not unfair allocation—is the cause of the shortage. And, significantly, the two policy issues—how best to procure organs and how best to allocate them—are, to a large degree, logically separable.[18]

Second, the primary emphasis throughout this study will be on the economics of the shortage and the competing policy alternatives to resolve it. A shortage is, by definition, an excess of quantity demanded over quantity supplied at the prevailing price. As such, a shortage is a distinctly economic phenomenon.[19] While economists certainly do not hold a monopoly on novel approaches to public policy issues, they do have a comparative advantage in analyzing the forces of supply and demand. And it is precisely those forces that principally underlie the organ—or any other—shortage. Consequently, economics is likely to provide the fundamental insights that, ultimately, hold the key to correct the current untenable situation. Specifically, a simple, straightforward economic analysis of the existing organ shortage and the various policy alternatives that have been proposed to resolve it provides the most promising approach to effective reform of organ procurement policy. Consequently, our principal focus in this monograph will be on the economic causes of and solutions to the organ shortage.[20]

Third, primarily for expositional convenience, we will place somewhat greater emphasis on kidneys as opposed to other transplantable organs.[21] This concentration on a single organ is necessary to apply the basic economic concepts of supply and demand, on which our analysis depends. Because different organs cannot be substituted for one another, one cannot legitimately draw a generalized demand curve for all transplantable organs.

We select the kidney as our model organ for two reasons. First, not only was this the first organ to be transplanted successfully, but it is also the organ for which the greatest demand for transplants—and, accordingly, the greatest shortage—currently exists. And second, virtually all organ collection activities currently revolve around kidney procurements. The End Stage Renal Disease Program, which is a part of Medicare, currently funds all organ procurement organizations in the United States, and almost all cadaveric organs collected are located through those organizations. As a result, heart, liver, lung, and other organ donations tend to occur in conjunction with efforts to acquire kidneys.[22] Importantly, however, our focus on kidneys does not preclude extension of our essential findings to other organs. With a few obvious modifications, our analysis applies directly to other transplantable organs, and our conclusions are valid for those organs as well.[23] An analysis of kidney procurement represents a useful test case, the conclusions from which can be applied to all transplantable organs.

Finally, we also limit our focus to cadaveric donorship or supply of organs. While living donors may provide certain nonessential or reproducible body parts (for example, a single kidney, a partial liver, or bone marrow), the bulk of the vital organ supply ultimately must come from cadavers. Moreover, with a more effective procurement system, cadaveric organ supply appears fully capable of meeting the entire demand for transplantable organs. This focus also obviates some of the more controversial ethical issues associated with organ supply from living donors and permits us to direct our attention to the policy options available for recovering transplantable organs from deceased individuals.[24] Given that focus, we turn to consider the economics and, to a limited extent, the ethics of alternative organ procurement policies.

2

The Organ Shortage:
A Brief History of a Policy Failure

People die for lack of those organs, but the legal system treats those organs as having no value.

—Fred H. Cate[1]

The existing organ shortage has grown from a public policy that was devised and implemented more by historical accident than by conscious design. Specifically, the earliest transplants were performed by using kidneys donated by living relatives of the recipients. At that time, transplantation technology—in particular, the state of knowledge regarding immunosuppressive therapy—effectively excluded cadaveric organ donors. As a result, organ transplant candidates, in effect, brought the necessary donor with them when they checked into the hospital for the transplant operation. If there was no acceptable living donor, no transplant operation was possible. Consequently, there were no waiting lists and no apparent shortage.

Moreover, under the living related donor system, no obvious need existed for any payment to encourage donor cooperation. The affection associated with the kinship between the donor and recipient was generally thought to be sufficient to motivate the requisite organ supply. And, where it was not, any necessary payment (or coercion) between family members could easily be arranged without resorting to the sort of middlemen generally required for market exchange. Such intrafamily cajoling by emotional pressure or outright payment or both also remained out of sight of the transplant centers and attending physicians. Therefore, a system of "altruistic" supply seemed to make sense in such a setting, and reliance on such a system did not seriously impede the use of that emerging medical technology.

The situation gradually changed, however, as new drugs, improved tissue matching, and advanced surgical procedures began to allow transplantation of cadaveric organs and simultaneously improved transplant success rates. Significantly, the new-found ability to make use of cadaveric organs expanded the application of transplant technology to vital organs other than kidneys. Although we have not been able to locate reliable data to pinpoint a precise time, probably sometime during the 1970s organ waiting lists began to appear as transplant candidates began to form queues for cadaveric organs. Those queues were generally managed by the transplant physicians located at the center where the operation was to be performed.

Before that time, in 1972, Congress established the End Stage Renal Disease Program. That program provided federal funding for kidney patients, including both dialysis services and renal transplants. Such funding undoubtedly increased the effective demand for kidney transplants both by providing third-party payment and by keeping many more potential transplant recipients alive for much longer periods of time through dialysis treatments. In addition, during the mid-1980s, private insurance companies increasingly began to provide coverage for other organ transplants (hearts, livers, etc.) as these procedures moved from the experimental stage to become accepted medical treatments.[2]

The clear impact of those developments has been the appearance and subsequent growth of an observable shortage of cadaveric organs. Despite the shortage, however, the basic public policy that had been inherited from the former days of living related donor transplants has never been seriously questioned or systematically evaluated. In fact, in 1984 Congress codified that de facto policy into law through passage of the National Organ Transplant Act, which explicitly proscribes any payment to organ donors to encourage supply for purposes of transplantation.[3]

Interestingly, the 1984 act was passed in response to an entrepreneurial attempt by a Virginia physician to alleviate the growing organ shortage by brokering living-donor kidneys.[4] The medical community's outrage at that development and its stringent defense of the altruistic system then led to political pressure that resulted in passage of the legislation. Similar legislative action followed in many states. As a result, the altruistic system was firmly locked into place without any serious inquiry regarding its relative effectiveness in an environment of cadaveric donors.

Thus, an organ procurement policy that was more or less a natural component of a transplant system that focused exclusively on living related donors was institutionalized for a system that now relies primarily on cadaveric organs from unrelated—and generally unknown—donors. And that policy is unquestionably the root cause of the current organ shortage. It is past time for Congress to reexamine that policy seriously.

The Process of Cadaveric Organ Procurement

From a practical standpoint, procurement of organs from cadavers for use in transplantation currently involves several steps. First, suitable cadaveric donors must be identified. Such donors must have healthy, well-functioning organs and be free of infection at the time of their death. In addition, the donor organs must be free of cancer, because the use of post-transplant immunosuppressive therapy tends to accelerate progression of the disease. In the past, an age limit on donors was generally applied. That limit was increased from fifty to fifty-five during the mid-1990s to expand the potential organ supply. More recently, an explicit age limit has been dropped, and a more subjective case-by-case evaluation is used to screen for acceptable donor organs.

In practice, the above conditions require that the majority of cadaveric organs come from accident or stroke victims who have been declared brain dead. Because of those rather stringent requirements, it has been estimated that only about 1 percent of all deaths in the United States occur under circumstances that would allow the organs of the deceased to be used in transplantation. As a result, identification of those potential donors in a timely fashion is an important first step in the procurement process, and failure to do so undoubtedly results in a large number of potential donations going uncollected.[5]

Next, once a potential organ donor has been identified, permission of surviving family members is generally sought. Notably, under the Uniform Anatomical Gift Act of 1987, such permission is not required in cases where the decedent has signed an organ donor card or executed some other valid premortem statement indicating a desire to donate upon death. In fact, under the legislation, the hospital where the death occurs has an affirmative obligation to honor the donor's wishes and remove the organs if they are medically suitable for use in transplantation. In practice, however, permission of surviving family members is sought even in cases where a valid donor card is present; and, in clear violation of the 1987 act, the organs are not collected if the family denies consent.[6]

Thus, as a practical—though not legal—matter, the property rights to the organs of deceased individuals rest with the surviving family members. Any premortem decision of the deceased to donate organs upon death can be overridden by the family's wishes. In such an environment, then, donor cards, where they exist and are located, serve the more limited role of informing the family of their deceased relative's desire to have the organs donated. Those cards are not, however, controlling in the ultimate decision.[7]

Given the need to obtain the family's consent to cadaveric organ donation, the methods used in seeking that consent become extremely important in determining the success of the procurement process. Current regulations require that all families of recently deceased potential donors be approached for permission to remove the organs. Because that request is determinative, how it is made is crucial to the outcome. Specifically, several studies have shown that both the timing of the request and how the request is framed can have significant effects on observed consent rates.[8] Also, the party making the request—a physician, nurse, or organ procurement officer—tends to influence outcomes. In particular, a number of cases have been reported in which physicians or others have fulfilled the legal requirement that a request be made in a fashion that is either inept or intentionally designed to elicit a negative response.[9] Thus, while legislation can, perhaps, require that a request be made, it cannot require that the request be made in a sincere and competent fashion that is likely to elicit a consent to donate.

Given the above process, obviously several reasons exist for cadaveric organ donation to fail to occur. The potential organ donor may not be identified in time, the family of the deceased may not be asked to consent to organ removal, the request for consent may not be made in a competent manner, or the family may simply refuse.[10] A breakdown at any point in the process results in a failure to collect the organs. It is little wonder, then, that only about one-quarter to one-half of all potential donor deaths result in organ donations.

Legal and Institutional Setting

Three major pieces of legislation have largely defined the legal and institutional landscape pertaining to organ procurement activities in the United States.[11] The first was the Uniform Anatomical Gift Act, which was formulated by the National Conference of Commissioners on Uniform State Laws in 1968.[12] By 1973, every state and the District of Columbia had adopted a version of that law. That body of legislation was intended to help resolve the then emerging organ shortage by facilitating bequests by individuals before their death, thereby (hopefully) expanding the supply of cadaveric organs. Thus, state legislatures were the first political bodies to recognize the shortage and take policy action intended to resolve the shortage.

The 1968 Uniform Anatomical Gift Act contained two principal provisions intended to increase organ supply. First, it recognized the right of individuals to consent explicitly to postmortem organ donation before their death. Such consent could be provided through a will or an organ donor card signed by two witnesses. And second, where such a document has been executed, the act specifically rules out the need for hospitals to obtain permission from surviving family members before removing the organs of the deceased.[13] Only in situations where the decedent had neither executed such a directive nor explicitly objected to organ removal was the family to be allowed to make that decision. Thus, the 1968 Uniform Anatomical Gift Act attempted to assign primary property rights to cadaveric organs to the donor.

Interestingly, that body of legislation contains no provision prohibiting payments in exchange for consent from either the decedent or the family. Thus, the formation of cadaveric organ markets—either futures or spot—is not precluded by that legislation.

The second major piece of legislation is the National Organ Transplant Act, enacted by Congress and signed by President Ronald

Reagan in 1984.[14] That act contains three principal objectives. First, as with the 1968 Uniform Anatomical Gift Act, the legislation was intended to help alleviate the by then large and growing shortage of cadaveric organs by expanding the available supply. Second, that act also sought to address increasing concerns regarding the fairness of the organ allocation process that had arisen from perceptions that some patients on waiting lists had received preferential treatment.[15] Third, the National Organ Transplant Act was also aimed at preventing the formation of markets for organs from either cadaveric or living donors.

The first two purposes—increasing supply and ensuring an equitable allocation—were pursued through a number of provisions creating and funding a set of both public and private institutions that, it was hoped, would increase supply primarily through better education and coordination of organ procurement activities. At the same time, those institutions were authorized to design, implement, and enforce organ allocation rules that would facilitate sharing of available organs between transplant centers and distributing those organs to individual patients in a more evenhanded manner.[16]

Four such institutions have emerged under that and the subsequent legislation. First, the National Organ Transplant Act required the secretary of the Department of Health and Human Services to create a separate administrative unit within the agency to implement the provisions of the act. As a result, the Division of Organ Transplant was established. According to Cate, that division's three major activities involve: (1) administering contracts and grants to the private nonprofit organizations that operate the procurement and allocation system; (2) conducting educational activities intended to increase both public and professional awareness of organ donation; and (3) fostering research on organ donation and transplantation issues.[17]

Second, under the first of those three activities, the Division of Organ Transplant was authorized to provide funding for an Organ Procurement and Transplantation Network and a Scientific Registry of Transplant Recipients.[18] The former, the Organ Procurement and Transplantation Network, was charged with the task of creating a national listing of all patients who have been approved as transplant candidates and a computerized system that could allocate the organs collected to the patients on that list.[19] The latter, the Scientific Registry, created an ongoing database related to clinical aspects involving transplant recipients to facilitate evaluative research.

Third, the United Network for Organ Sharing, which is also a private, nonprofit organization funded by federal grants, carries out the Organ Procurement and Transplantation Network's organ procurement and allocation activities. As a member of the network, the United Network for Organ Sharing operates the computerized allocation system that assigns organs to patients on the basis of a formula that incorporates various criteria including, *inter alia,* the degree of tissue match, blood type, the patient's medical condition, and length of time on the list. The specific criteria used and the weights assigned to each vary somewhat across organs for medical reasons (for example, tissue typing is done for kidneys but not for hearts and livers). Policy changes affecting allocation decisions, then, are administered by United Network for Organ Sharing.

Fourth, under the National Organ Transplant Act, the Division of Organ Transplant is also authorized to provide grants to organ procurement organizations.[20] Those too are private, nonprofit organizations. They receive funding both from Division of Organ Transplant grants and from cost-based fees billed to transplant centers for the organs delivered to them.[21] To a large degree, the organ procurement organizations provide the cornerstone of the U.S. organ procurement system. Those organizations provide trained personnel who approach the families of recently deceased individuals who are potential organ donors.[22] Thus, the organ procurement organizations are on the "front lines" of the organ procurement system.

At this time the United States has approximately fifty-five to sixty organ procurement organizations. Their number varies somewhat over time as some exit the business or merge with other organ procurement organizations. Under federal rules, each organ procurement organization is assigned an exclusive geographic collection region. As a result, little, if any, competition exists among the organ procurement organizations for procurement activities.[23] Once the organization collects an organ, it is entered into the United Network for Organ Sharing system for allocation to a patient on the waiting list.

Finally, the National Organ Transplant Act's prohibition on organ sales is explicit. Specifically, the act makes it illegal to "knowingly acquire, receive, or otherwise transfer any human organ for valuable consideration for use in human transplantation."[24] Violation of that provision is a felony and can lead to a fine of up to $50,000 or a prison sentence of up to five years or both. The act goes on to specify, however, that "the term 'valuable consideration' does not include the reasonable payments associated with the removal, transportation, implantation, processing, preservation, quality control, and storage of a human organ."[25] Thus, as others have noted, while organ donors and their families are proscribed from receiving payment for their consent to remove the organs, all other parties involved in the production and supply of transplant services are exempted from the provision. They can all be paid.

The third major legislative effort to address the (still growing) organ shortage was the updated Uniform Anatomical Gift Act, which the National Conference of Commissioners on Uniform State Laws approved in 1987. That act differs from the 1968 Uniform Anatomical Gift Act in three primary respects. First, the new law requires hospitals to make a "routine inquiry" or "routine request" of each patient regarding his willingness to be an organ donor and to inquire whether the patient has previously executed an organ donor card. Second, the law instructs emergency personnel (for example, police, firefighters, and paramedics) to conduct a reasonable search for victims' donor cards. And third, following the National Organ Transplant Act, the 1987 Uniform Anatomical Gift Act proscribes organ purchases and sales. Like its predecessor, the recent act continues to place legal priority on the donor's wishes regarding organ removal over the preferences of surviving family members.

In addition to the above three major legislative efforts, the states have adopted a number of laws pertaining to organ procurement and allocation. Those laws generally correspond closely to the acts discussed above. Some notable departures exist, however. Most importantly, several states do not appear to proscribe organ sales. Within those states, then, the use of financial incentives to encourage donation might be legal if such incentives are judged to have no impact on interstate commerce.

Also, subsequent to the above legislative actions, other laws and regulations have helped shape the organ procurement process. Most notably, regulations issued by the Health Care Financing Administration in August 1998 require all hospitals receiving federal (including Medicare or Medicaid) funds to refer all in-hospital deaths to their regional organ procurement organization. Moreover, under those regulations, known as "required referral," deaths are supposed to be reported in a timely manner— that is, when death is imminent and before the respirator has been disconnected. In the vast majority of deaths, of course, the dying patients do not qualify as potential organ donors; and most of those can be screened out by the organ procurement organization from information provided over the phone. Where organ donation appears feasible, however, the organization's representative will go to the hospital to approach the family.[26]

Thus, the legal and institutional environment within which the organ procurement and transplant industry operates is rather complex. An interconnected system of public and private agencies interact to collect and allocate cadaveric organs, provide policy advice to legislative bodies, and implement any policy changes affecting how those activities are conducted. The system has been modified extensively over time in repeated attempts by legislators and regulators to improve performance. And, in a very limited sense, those efforts have had some degree of success—organ donations have increased. But the larger goal of satisfying the total demand for transplantable organs has consistently failed to be met.

The Organ Shortage: Fundamentals of Supply and Demand

Economists define a shortage as a condition in which the quantity of a product demanded exceeds the quantity supplied *at the existing price*. To appreciate what this definition implies for the organ shortage, one must first understand two fundamental aspects of the concepts of supply and demand. First, both of these concepts refer to *schedules* relating the quantities bought and sold to various prices paid and received. That is, the term *demand* means a schedule (which may be expressed in the form of a table, graph, or equation) that shows the quantities that will be purchased at all possible prices. A specific quantity at some point along that schedule is referred to as the *quantity demanded at the specified price*. Similarly, *supply* is a schedule that shows the quantities that will be placed on the market for sale at all possible prices. And *quantity supplied* refers to a single point along that schedule. Thus, the present shortage of transplantable organs is equal to the quantity demanded minus the quantity supplied at the current price of organs, which, under the existing policy, is zero.

Second, and extremely important for our discussion here, the quantities referred to in the definitions of both *supply* and *demand* are *flows,* not stocks. In other words, those quantities are expressed as some number of units of the product *per some interval of time.* To say that the quantity demanded or supplied of product X is 100 units at a price of $10 per unit is meaningless unless we specify the time period over which those 100 units will be purchased or sold. Is it a week, a month, a year, or a decade? Obviously, the demand and supply of a product will vary substantially depending on the time interval over which they are defined.

This second point is crucial to understand, because it has been the source of considerable confusion in debates about the organ shortage and alternative policies to resolve it. Specifically, participants in these debates often have explicitly or implicitly confused the number of patients on transplant waiting lists (which is a stock) with the concept of a shortage (which is a flow).[27] The size of the waiting lists for transplantable organs represents the accumulation of the shortages of all preceding periods, adjusted for the attrition that occurs from patients' dying. As such, observed waiting lists greatly exaggerate the magnitude of the actual organ shortage on an annual basis.

For example, at the current price, table 2-1 indicates that in 1998 we had an annual shortage (adjusted for deaths) of 6,423 kidneys (or 4,128 if we do not adjust for deaths).[28] Then, if we assume no attrition from deaths and the shortage remains at that level, the waiting list for kidney transplants will grow at a rate of 6,423 patients per year, so that at the end of five years the waiting list will have grown by 32,115 patients to 74,479.

Table 2-1 Waiting Lists, Deaths, and Shortages: Kidneys

Year	Transplants Cadaveric	Transplants Living	Patients on waiting list	Increase in waiting list (annual)	% Increase in waiting list	Deaths on waiting list[a]	Increase in deaths on waiting list	% Increase in deaths on waiting list	Annual shortage including deaths
1988	7,231	1,812	13,943			734			
1989	7,087	1,903	16,294	2,351	17	749	15	2	3,100
1990	7,782	2,094	17,883	1,589	10	916	167	22	2,505
1991	7,733	2,393	19,352	1,469	8	974	58	6	2,443
1992	7,696	2,536	22,376	3,024	16	1,047	73	7	4,071
1993	8,171	2,850	24,973	2,597	12	1,277	230	22	3,874
1994	8,384	3,008	27,498	2,525	10	1,365	88	7	3,890
1995	8,602	3,347	31,045	3,547	13	1,503	138	10	5,050
1996	8,571	3,605	34,550	3,505	11	1,802	299	20	5,307
1997	8,613	3,797	38,236	3,686	11	1,989	187	10	5,675
1998	8,938	4,017	42,364	4,128	11	2,295	306	15	6,423
% Change 1988 to 1998	24		204	796		213	1,940		107

a. Number of patients who died while on a transplant waiting list.
Source: www.unos.org/Newsroom/critdata_transplants_ustx.htm.

The kidney *shortage,* however, is not 74,479 organs per year. To see this, suppose that an additional 74,479 kidneys per year were suddenly to become available. In that event, the waiting list (or backlog) could be completely eliminated within the first or second year, and a surplus of over 68,000 kidneys would then appear in all subsequent years. Rather, despite the current waiting list of 42,364 patients, an increase in the quantity of kidneys supplied of only 6,423 per year would eliminate the *annual* shortage and, with no attrition, would maintain the waiting list at the current level of 42,364 patients. Given the backlog of excess demand that has accumulated from past shortages, however, an increase in the quantity supplied of, say, 20,000 kidneys per year would immediately eliminate the annual shortage and would also eliminate the backlog within three to four years. Thus, it is essential to understand the distinction between waiting lists and shortages (stocks and flows) in any discussions concerning the magnitude of the organ shortage.[29]

With that distinction and our prior definitions in mind, what can a basic economic analysis tell us about the organ shortage? To answer that question, we need to construct the supply and demand curves for a particular transplantable organ. As noted above, we use kidneys to illustrate the fundamental points. Figure 2-1 depicts what we believe are reasonable approximations to the relevant supply and demand curves for kidneys.

As drawn, the curves shown in the figure exhibit two empirical facts that we know with relative certainty about the market for kidneys as well as two additional characteristics suggested by some rather straightforward economic reasoning. First, turning to the facts, table 2-1 indicates that in 1998 the supply curve of cadaveric kidneys had a horizontal intercept of 8,938. That is simply the number of cadaveric kidneys that donors were willing to supply at the legal price of zero. Second, table 2-1 also indicates that, at this zero price, the total quantity of kidneys demanded (both cadaveric and living) for transplantation in 1998 was 19,378 (which is the number of cadaveric kidneys supplied, 8,938, plus the number of living-donor kidneys supplied, 4,017, plus the remaining shortage, 6,423). Together, those two facts indicate that the shortage of cadaveric kidneys in 1998 was 10,440 (or a shortage of cadaveric donors of slightly over 5,220).[30]

Figure 2-1 The Supply and Demand Curves for Kidneys from Cadaveric Donors

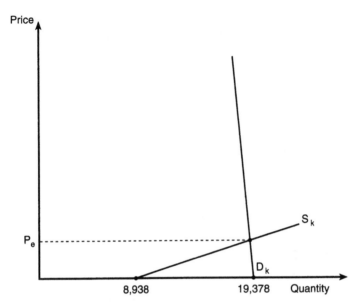

Next, the supply and demand curves drawn here exhibit slopes that we think are suggested by the economic characteristics of this market. First, the demand curve is drawn with an extremely steep slope (or a very low price elasticity of demand). That aspect of our graph indicates that purchasers of cadaveric kidneys are not likely to reduce substantially the number of kidneys demanded as the price rises above zero, at least over some relatively wide range of positive prices. The expectation of a highly price inelastic demand is founded on two important—and, we believe, noncontroversial—aspects regarding this good. First, while dialysis is a substitute for a kidney transplant, for many patients it is a relatively poor substitute.[31] And second, because kidney transplants are covered under the End Stage Renal Disease Program, all (or virtually all) kidney transplants are subject to third-party payment, which typically results in low price elasticities of demand. Together, those considerations suggest an extremely steep (or inelastic) demand curve, as we have drawn here.

At the same time, we have drawn the cadaveric kidney supply curve with a relatively small slope. This slope suggests that potential suppliers of cadaveric kidneys—either the donors themselves with a futures type premortem agreement to supply or the donors' surviving family members in the absence of such a supply contract—are likely to increase substantially the number of organs supplied as the price is increased above zero. That is, we have assumed a relatively large price elasticity of supply. That assumption, while less certain than our assumption regarding the price elasticity of demand, is also founded on two straightforward economic considerations.

First, as noted earlier, we are currently collecting a fairly small percentage (probably no more than a third and certainly less than half) of the cadaveric organs that potentially could be acquired and used in transplant procedures.[32] As a result, it would be possible to expand greatly the number of cadaveric kidneys supplied without confronting the "capacity constraint" provided by available suitable organs. Indeed, the figures reported in table 2-1 indicate that the cadaveric kidney shortage could be eliminated entirely by expanding collections from 8,938 to 19,378 kidneys, which, if there are, say, only 15,000 potential donors (supplying slightly less than two kidneys each), would still represent a collection rate of approximately 70 percent. Thus, a significant expansion in the number of cadaveric kidneys supplied is clearly feasible.

Second, for most potential cadaveric organ donors, we expect that the opportunity cost of supplying the organs is rather low. Generally organ removal causes no visible disfigurement to the body (indeed, open-casket funerals can still be held), and the only apparent alternative use is to bury the cadaver with the organs in place. Or, as some in the transplant community have graphically stated it, to "feed them to the worms." For most (though certainly not all) potential donors, such use is not likely to be valued highly.[33] Thus, with substantial excess capacity and low opportunity costs for most potential suppliers, it seems reasonable to expect a relatively price elastic cadaveric organ supply curve over a fairly wide range of prices above zero.[34]

To the extent that figure 2-1 accurately portrays the supply and demand curves for cadaveric kidneys, we may draw two important conclusions. First, and most important, the simple analysis presented above suggests that the fundamental cause of the long-standing shortage of cadaveric organs made available for transplantation is our current policy that prohibits payments to organ donors and effectively sets the legal price at zero. In the absence of that policy, shortage conditions would cause the market price to be bid upward to its equilibrium level, which is shown as P_e in the graph. At that price, the quantity supplied is equal to the quantity demanded, and the shortage disappears. That is *the* fundamental lesson that economics offers regarding this important public policy issue. The only reason we have an organ shortage is our insistence that potential cadaveric organ suppliers cannot be paid. And as long as that policy remains in place, efforts to eliminate the shortage are likely to continue to fail.[35]

Second, to the extent that our economic reasoning regarding the price elasticity of supply of cadaveric organs is correct, the equilibrium, market-clearing price of cadaveric organs is likely to be relatively low. Of course, we cannot provide an empirical estimate of that price on the basis of figure 2-1, but the underlying economics would tend to suggest that this price is not high. This (tentative) conclusion, if correct, will be shown to have important implications for many of the arguments—both economic and ethical—that have been raised in ongoing debates about alternative methods to resolve the organ shortage.

On this last point, it is crucial to distinguish the equilibrium market price, P_e, from a black-market price that might prevail in the absence of legal market exchange. Several authors who have written in this area have either explicitly or implicitly assumed that a high price would emerge with organ markets.[36] Where shortage conditions prevail and, particularly, where market demand is highly price inelastic, the black-market price is likely to exceed the equilibrium price by a considerable margin.

Consider figure 2-2. Here, we have redrawn figure 2-1 with two modifications. First, we have added living donors to the supply curve, which shifts the horizontal intercept to the right by 4,017 kidneys (the number indicated in table 2-1). Thus, that intercept is now equal to 12,955, which is the total number of kidney transplants performed in 1998. And second, we have made the demand curve slightly more price elastic to obtain a black-market price that can easily be shown on the

Figure 2-2 Equilibrium versus Black-Market Prices

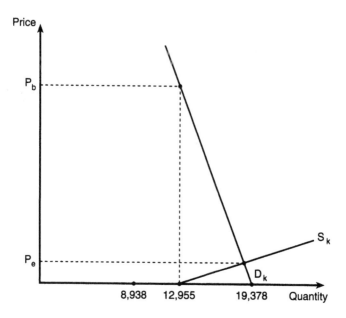

graph.[37] Neither of those modifications is crucial to the point we make here.

Given the supply and demand curves shown in figure 2-2, we show (consistent with table 2-1) a shortage of 6,423 (19,378 minus 12,955) kidneys at a price of zero. Given that shortage, the black-market price is shown as P_b, and that price greatly exceeds the market-clearing price of P_e (here, by a factor of about ten).[38] The large difference between black-market and equilibrium prices reflects the combined effects of: (1) the restriction in the quantity supplied caused by the legal price constraint; and (2) the highly price-inelastic demand. In effect, the black-market price simply bears testament to the desperation of those patients who are affluent enough to pay relatively high prices to obtain needed organs but are not allowed to do so legally under the existing policy.

The important point for our purposes here and at various points throughout this monograph is that P_b should not be confused with P_e. That is, an observed willingness of some patients to pay, say, $40,000 or more for a kidney under the existing shortage conditions does not indicate that market-clearing prices will be anywhere near that range.[39] Given the economic characteristics that underlie the supply and demand curves that are likely to apply, P_e is virtually certain to fall well short of P_b.

Finally, note that in figures 2-1 and 2-2 the equilibrium, market-clearing quantity of kidneys procured falls slightly below the quantity demanded at the zero price (19,378). This feature of those graphs would appear to suggest that, under a market system of procurement, all patients who would benefit medically from an organ transplant would not be able to receive one, even though, from an economic perspective, the shortage is eliminated.[40] Two considerations, however, suggest that such rationing of patients out of the market does not present a serious concern. First, and most obvious, the equilibrium quantity greatly exceeds the current, supply-restricted quantity. Thus, many more patients would receive transplants under a market system of procurement than currently receive them with reliance entirely on altruistic supply. And second, to the extent that third-party payment is available to all transplant patients, the organ demand curve is likely to be vertical (that is, perfectly price inelastic) over the relevant price range (0 to P_e). As a result, all patients who would benefit medically from a transplant will receive one.

Organ Shortages: Magnitudes and Trends. In light of the foregoing definitions and analysis, how large is the organ shortage and at what rate is it and the backlog (waiting list) growing? Given the prominence of this issue in public policy forums over the past decade, one would think that reliable information would be readily available. Amazingly, however, the data are quite sparse. The information we were able to locate is deficient in at least two respects. First, no direct evidence exists on the annual shortages of transplantable organs (although one can obtain approximations of those shortages from information relating to the observed changes in the size of waiting lists). And second, the evidence that is available does not cover an extended period of time (going back only to December 1987).

With those deficiencies in mind, tables 2-1, 2-2, and 2-3 present the best information we could find regarding the magnitude of the shortages for the three most widely transplanted organs—kidneys, livers, and

Table 2-2 Waiting Lists, Deaths, and Shortages: Livers

Year	Transplants Cadaveric	Transplants Living	Patients on waiting list	Increase in waiting (annual) list	% Increase in waiting list	Deaths on waiting list[a]	Increase in deaths on waiting list	% Increase in deaths on waiting list	Annual shortage including deaths
1988	1,713	0	616			196			
1989	2,199	2	827	211	34	282	86	44	493
1990	2,677	14	1,237	410	50	317	35	12	727
1991	2,931	22	1,676	439	35	435	118	37	874
1992	3,031	33	2,323	647	39	495	60	14	1,142
1993	3,404	36	2,997	674	29	560	65	13	1,234
1994	3,592	60	4,059	1,062	35	655	95	17	1,717
1995	3,879	46	5,691	1,632	40	797	142	22	2,429
1996	4,013	53	7,467	1,776	31	956	159	20	2,732
1997	4,101	69	9,637	2,170	29	1,130	174	18	3,300
1998	4,384	66	12,056	2,419	25	1,319	189	17	3,738
% Change 1988 to 1998	156		1,857	1,046		573	120		658

a. Number of patients who died while on a transplant waiting list.
Source: www.unos.org/Newsroom/critdata_transplants_ustx.htm.

Table 2-3 Waiting Lists, Deaths, and Shortages: Hearts

Year	Transplants Cadaveric	Transplants Living[a]	Patients on waiting list	Increase in waiting list (annual)	% Increase in waiting list	Deaths on waiting list[b]	Increase in deaths on waiting list	% Increase in deaths on waiting list	Annual shortage including deaths
1988	1,670	7	1,010			493			807
1989	1,696	9	1,320	290	28	517	24	5	1,081
1990	2,095	12	1,788	468	35	613	96	19	1,257
1991	2,122	4	2,267	479	27	778	165	27	1,202
1992	2,170	1	2,690	423	19	779	1	0	
1993	2,295	2	2,834	144	5	761	-18	-2	905
1994	2,338	3	2,933	99	3	724	-37	-5	823
1995	2,361	0	3,468	535	18	769	45	6	1,304
1996	2,342	1	3,698	230	7	745	-24	-3	975
1997	2,294	0	3,897	199	5	772	27	4	971
1998	2,340	0	4,184	287	7	767	-5	-1	1,055
% Change 1988 to 1998		306	306	1,046		56	-121		31

a. Living heart donors donate their healthy heart when they become heart-lung recipients.
b. Number of patients who died while on a transplant waiting list.
Source: www.unos.org/Newsroom/critdata_transplants_ustx.htm.

hearts. In those tables, we have calculated two alternative estimates of the annual shortages. Both are based on simple differences in the waiting lists from one year to the next. One is adjusted for waiting list attrition due to deaths, while the other is not. Because some, but not all, deaths of individuals on organ waiting lists are due to the inability to obtain a suitable organ in time, only a portion of those deaths is likely to be attributable to the shortage itself. That is, some, but not all, of those lives could have been saved if transplantable organs had been more readily available. As a result, the figures reported in those two measures of the shortage for each organ are likely to bracket the true annual shortages to the extent that the waiting lists approximate the actual number of potential transplant recipients (more on this below).

For kidneys, one can divide the differences by a factor of slightly less than two to reflect the fact that, in most cases (generally between 80 and 90 percent), two kidneys can be recovered from a single cadaver. Those adjusted figures, then, would provide a rough estimate of the annual kidney shortage in terms of the number of additional donors needed.[41] Obviously, a similar adjustment for other organs is not required.

Importantly, the numbers reported in tables 2-1, 2-2, and 2-3 are apt to understate the actual shortage of organs, perhaps by a considerable margin. Specifically, it is likely that the reported waiting lists from which we have calculated our implied shortages understate the number of patients for whom an organ transplant is a viable and beneficial treatment option. It appears that some patients are denied admission to those waiting lists at least in part because of the shortage itself. All potential transplant candidates undergo screening by transplant physicians before their being placed on organ waiting lists. Such screening has almost certainly become more stringent as those lists have grown, and patients who might have been judged to be viable transplant candidates under less restrictive organ supply conditions may increasingly be denied access to that form of treatment by a refusal to approve them for placement on the list.[42] That is, the stringency of the screening criteria is likely to have increased as the waiting lists have grown.[43] Thus, it is quite likely that the figures reported in tables 2-1, 2-2, and 2-3 provide downward-biased estimates of both the potential waiting lists and the implied annual shortages. The magnitude of those biases, however, cannot be determined with currently available data.

Given that caveat, tables 2-1, 2-2, and 2-3 provide some interesting observations regarding the organ shortage. First, focusing on the deaths-adjusted figures, we see that the magnitude of the annual shortages for both kidneys and livers has grown substantially over the 1988–1998 period. Specifically, the annual shortage of kidneys has risen 107 percent, and the annual shortage of livers has risen over 650 percent. Those rising annual shortages, then, have led to an exponential growth in observed waiting lists (over 200 percent for kidneys and almost 2,000 percent for livers over the 1988–1998 period). While the growth of those shortages has not always been continuous, the upward trend is obvious.

That conclusion, however, does not apply to hearts. Here, the annual shortages, disregarding deaths on the waiting list, have been relatively flat, with some upward and downward movements over that interval. Including deaths on the waiting list, the shortage of hearts has increased by only 31 percent since 1988. As a result, the waiting list for hearts has grown steadily, but at a linear rather than an exponential rate. Nonetheless, the waiting list for hearts has increased by 306 percent over the 1988–1998 period.

Perhaps the most important lesson to be gleaned from the three tables is that the organ shortage is clearly not a recent phenomenon. For as far back as we have reliable data, an organ shortage has always existed.[44] That is, the current, so-called altruistic system of organ procurement has consistently failed to yield an adequate supply of any of these transplantable organs. Despite increased efforts to make the system work—through heightened spending on donor education, adoption of less stringent donor requirements, enactment of required request laws, implementation of required referral regulations, and so on—it has never yielded sufficient organs to meet the needs of patients. As a result, well-meaning appeals to resolve the organ shortage through policies that continue to rely on this basic system by modifying it in various nonfundamental ways—for example, by spending more on education or allowing directed giving, where donors are allowed to have some control over which recipients will receive the organs—should not be expected to produce profound effects.[45] While such modifications may increase organ supply somewhat, they are not likely to eliminate the shortage.[46] To the extent that such policy recommendations are adopted in lieu of more fundamental changes, they will only condemn more patients to death as they postpone more meaningful reforms.

Finally, we must emphasize that, while the distinction between shortages and waiting lists is important in understanding the organ procurement problem and the policy mechanisms to resolve it, the growth in waiting lists is creating severe repercussions in terms of death and human suffering. That is, the undesirable consequences of a shortage (which we describe below) tend to mount as that shortage persists over time, even if the shortage itself is constant. Whether a shortage is large or small, increasing or decreasing, the harms it creates will continue to expand as long as any shortage remains.

Thus, little or no comfort should be taken from the fact that the annual shortage of a particular organ has not been rising steadily in recent years. The increase in the waiting lists means that patients will experience increasingly prolonged suffering, declining health, and rising death rates as long as those shortages persist. We turn now to examine the causes and consequences of the organ shortage.

Causes of the Shortage

Two of the most fundamental laws of economics are the laws of supply and demand. The former law states that, as the price of a good increases, the number of units placed on the market for sale will also increase. In other words, the supply curve slopes upward. The latter law states that, as the price of a good increases, the number of units purchased will fall. In other words, the demand curve slopes downward.[47] Those laws are reflected in the supply and demand curves depicted in figures 2-1 and 2-2.

Given those economic laws and the definition of a shortage as the difference between the quantity demanded and the quantity supplied at a given price, then, the cause of any shortage is a price that falls below the equilibrium, market-clearing level and (for whatever reason) is not permitted to rise. The organ shortage is no exception. As noted above, first by convention and later by legislation, the price of all organs for transplantation (both from living and cadaveric donors) has been set at zero. Since organ transplantation first became feasible in the late 1950s, the existing policy has required that organ acquisition occur through donation rather than sale. As noted above, that policy was codified in 1984 by the National Organ Transplant Act, which makes it a felony to buy or sell human organs for the purpose of transplantation.[48] That legislation has served to codify the de facto policy that had already been put in place by transplant physicians requiring that the transfer occur at a price of zero.

As a consequence of that public policy, organ suppliers—who, for cadaveric organs, are generally the families of critically injured accident victims—are not allowed to receive any financial compensation in exchange for granting permission to remove the organs of their recently deceased relatives. Therefore, their decision to allow such removal under the existing system must be based entirely on their altruistic desire to supply needed organs to unknown recipients awaiting transplantation.[49] Altruism is thus the sole motivating force behind organ supply under the current system.

Importantly, a direct consequence of that policy is to prevent any sort of commercial brokerage activity in organs from arising. Indeed, prevention of such activity appears to be the principal motivating factor behind that policy and the body of legislation that supports it.[50] By outlawing brokers, however, the policy also limits the direct financial incentive for hospitals or other parties actively and effectively to seek out cadaveric organs for use in transplantation. Unless the hospital in which the potential organ donor dies houses an active transplant center, that hospital has little or no financial incentive to request organ donation from the families of recently deceased patients, because such organs cannot be resold.[51] Also (and, perhaps, more importantly), the proscription on brokerage severely limits the incentive mechanisms that organ procurement organizations can use to encourage increased donations. Specifically, by outlawing the use of financial incentives to elicit improved response rates among families of potential organ donors, those organizations are forced to rely on families' altruistic inclinations alone. Thus, the current (zero price) policy proscribing the use of financial incentives adversely affects the decisions both to agree to supply and actively to acquire cadaveric organs for transplantation. Consequently, the chronic shortage of transplantable organs can be laid squarely at the feet of that public policy.

While the current policy's sole reliance on altruistic supply is the fundamental cause of the shortage of organs, three additional factors have contributed to the persistent and growing excess demand. First, a number of significant technological advances have occurred that have markedly improved the success rates of organ transplantation and have thereby shifted the demand for transplants and transplantable organs outward. As noted earlier, the principal discovery contributing to the improvement in transplant technology has been cyclosporine, an immunosuppressive drug that substantially reduces the risk of rejection of the transplanted organ.[52] That drug was introduced in the United States in 1983 and has been successfully applied to, among others, kidney, heart, and liver transplants.[53] Overall success rates for transplants of those three organs are 85 percent, 80 percent, and 50–70 percent, respectively,[54] which compare quite favorably with the precyclosporine success rates of approximately 70 percent for kidneys, 58 percent for hearts, and 25 percent for livers.[55]

Second, a 1972 amendment to the Social Security Act authorizes the federal government to pay 80 percent of the cost of treatment (including both dialysis and transplantation) of all persons suffering from kidney failure.[56] Such payment occurs under the End Stage Renal Disease Program, which is operated under Medicare. Expenditures under that program have grown from $228.5 million in 1974 to over $6 billion in 1998. In addition, private insurance coverage has gradually expanded to include heart, liver, and other transplants as those procedures have become increasingly commonplace. Those increases in government funding and private insurance coverage have further stimulated the growth in transplant demand.

Third, after years of continual growth at approximately 10 percent per year, cadaveric kidney donations abruptly leveled off in 1986 and have exhibited substantially slower growth rates since that time.[57] The cause of that sudden change in the trend in cadaveric organ donation has been subject to considerable debate, but no one has yet provided a definitive answer. Moreover, the decline has occurred despite substantial increases in federal funding of organ procurement since enactment of the

National Organ Transplant Act of 1984.[58] The decline has also occurred despite a liberalization of the criteria applied to potential donors (for example, an increase in the maximum age of individuals from whom organs could be removed for transplantation).[59] The chronically inadequate supply of transplantable organs also persists despite the expenditure of several hundred million dollars annually by the Health Care Financing Administration on organ procurement efforts.

Also, significantly, the shortfall in supply persists despite the fact that the number of potential donors exceeds the number of organs needed annually. In 1989 Prottas estimated that between 17,000 and 26,000 people die annually under circumstances that would permit organ donation.[60] Other, more recent estimates suggest a lower figure.[61] Nonetheless, as shown in table 2-4, 8,938 kidneys were transplanted from 5,327 cadaveric donors in 1998. Those figures suggest that somewhere between 20 and 50 percent of potential donations currently result in actual donations. On that basis, then, a doubling or tripling of the number of kidney transplants could occur within the constraint provided by the number of deaths of potential organ donors.[62]

In sum, the current organ shortage results from an insufficient rate of donation or collection under the present altruistic policy. It does not result from an inadequate supply of potential organ donors. Therefore, the organ shortage we are experiencing is not mandated by nature. Rather, it is the outcome of a myopic public policy that provides insufficient incentives for cadaveric organ donation to occur.[63]

Consequences of the Shortage

The most direct and obvious consequence of the failure of the quantity of organs supplied to equal the quantity demanded is the appearance and subsequent growth of organ waiting lists. As the organ shortage has persisted over time and those lists have grown, a number of other associated consequences have emerged that have imposed substantial costs (both public and private, monetary and emotional) on society. We describe some of the more egregious adverse effects of the organ shortage here.

Table 2-4 Number of Cadaveric Kidney Transplants, Donors, and Transplants per Donor

	1988	1989	1990	1991	1992	1993	1994	1995	1996	1997	1998
Cadaveric transplants	7,231	7,087	7,782	7,733	7,696	8,171	8,384	8,602	8,571	8,613	8,938
Cadaveric donors	3,876	3,810	4,306	4,268	4,276	4,609	4,798	5,001	5,037	5,082	5,327
Transplants/ donor (percent)	1.866	1.860	1.807	1.812	1.800	1.773	1.747	1.720	1.702	1.695	1.678

Sources: www.unos.org/Newsroom/critdata_donors.htm; and www.unos.org/Newsroom/critdata_transplants_ustx.htm.

Table 2-5 Median Waiting Times (in Days) to Transplant

Year	Kidney	Liver	Heart
1988	400	34	116
1989	460	39	137
1990	484	45	165
1991	535	66	199
1992	618	104	244
1993	722	140	210
1994	828	163	180
1995	962	247	209
1996	n.a.	367	224
1997	n.a.	477	207

n.a. = not available.

Source: www.unos.org/Data/anrpt98.

Length of Waiting Times. First, the expansion of organ waiting lists has translated directly into longer waiting times for patients needing transplants. While the data here are somewhat limited, the evidence that is available reveals that, for all three organs examined, waiting times have increased substantially. Table 2-5 shows a 141 percent increase in waiting times for kidneys in only seven years. Specifically, the median wait for renal patients has risen from just over one year to 2.6 years over this period. And waiting times for hearts and livers increased over 78 percent and 1,300 percent over a nine-year period, respectively.

The lengthening of waiting times for transplant candidates has at least three serious consequences. First, both patient suffering and the considerable expense of keeping those patients alive while they wait for an organ are prolonged. Second, the patients' health often deteriorates as time passes, so that they are less able to withstand the physical stress of the transplant operation, a factor that reduces success rates. And third, many of those patients die as a direct consequence of the inability to obtain a suitable organ for transplantation within a shorter time period.

Tables 2-1, 2-2, and 2-3, presented earlier, document the number of deaths of patients on transplant waiting lists for kidneys, livers, and hearts over the 1988–1998 period. The most recent figure for all transplant candidates is 6,012 deaths in 1999.[64] Several points are worth noting here. First, the figures reported are simply the number of people who died while on an official waiting list in the given year. Obviously, transplantation could not have prevented all of those deaths. On this score, then, the figures tend to overstate the number of deaths attributable to the organ shortage.

Other considerations, however, suggest that those numbers may seriously understate the true consequences of the shortage. For example, some patients die without ever being placed on a waiting list. At least some of those patients' lives might have been saved by a transplant. In addition, a large number of patients are removed from waiting lists because they become too sick to undergo the transplant operation. A large portion of them die shortly after being removed from the list. As a result, the number of patients who die while on transplant waiting lists understates the number who die as a consequence of the shortage, perhaps by a substantial margin. The figures in our tables do not account for this; therefore, we cannot say with certainty just how many patients are dying as a result of the shortage of transplantable organs. We can say, however, that it runs into the thousands each year and is growing rapidly as the lists themselves continue to grow. And the death toll continues to mount over time as policymakers insist that we continue to rely solely upon altruistic supply for organ procurement.

Increasing Use of Dialysis. A second major consequence of the organ shortage is to expand greatly the number of renal patients whose lives are sustained through dialysis. At present, approximately 185,000 patients are receiving dialysis treatments in the United States.[65] Of those patients, only about 45,000 (or 24 percent) appear on the official waiting list for a kidney transplant. Prottas has estimated that as many as one-half of all dialysis patients would be suitable candidates for a transplant in the absence of a shortage.[66] While that estimate may be somewhat inflated, it is nonetheless clear that many patients could be removed from dialysis if the organ shortage were eliminated.

Two important social costs are associated with maintaining those patients on dialysis. First, dialysis is a more expensive treatment for renal failure than transplantation. Research indicates that a successful kidney transplant saves as much as $60,000 per patient over a five-year period compared with dialysis costs over the same period.[67] As noted above, those costs are paid by the Health Care Financing Administration under the End Stage Renal Disease Program. Thus, if the entire waiting list of over 40,000 renal patients could be transplanted, the program would reduce costs by more than $2.4 billion over a five-year period. Arguably, those savings could more than double if all renal patients who might benefit from a kidney transplant received a successful donor organ. The inability to achieve that cost reduction is directly attributable to the shortage of kidneys for transplantation created by the current procurement system.

Furthermore, although dialysis is capable of sustaining indefinitely a renal patient's life, it is far from a perfect substitute for a successful kidney transplant. Patients on dialysis must spend a considerable amount of time connected to the dialysis machine.[68] Moreover, many (or most) of those patients experience energy loss, nausea, weakness, hypertension, bone disease, infections, atherosclerotic disease, and other problems that emanate from the treatment itself. As a result, many (or most) of those patients are unable to work and experience substantial reductions in income and their overall quality of life.[69] While those costs do not appear on any formal ledger, they are, nonetheless, very real to the patients who must bear them.

Finally, recent evidence indicates that renal patients who have never been placed on dialysis experience a significantly lower risk of rejecting the transplanted organ than patients who have undergone dialysis treatments, at least for living-donor transplants.[70] Moreover, for most kidney transplant candidates, dialysis is necessary only because a cadaveric organ cannot be located more promptly. Thus, by forcing patients to go on dialysis for a period of time before receiving transplants, the cadaveric organ shortage causes a heightened rate of transplant rejections. The rejected organs, in turn, are wasted and patients' suffering and risk of death are increased.

Reliance on Living Donors. A third major consequence of the chronic shortage of cadaveric organs is an increasing reliance on living donors.

Although living donors have been used to a very limited extent for lung and liver transplants, the principal organ for which live donation is feasible is the kidney. As mentioned earlier, the first kidney transplants were performed exclusively with living related donors. As cadaveric donation became feasible, physicians continued to rely somewhat on living related donors for kidney transplants largely because of the higher success rates experienced. The success rate differential between living and cadaveric kidneys, however, has narrowed as significant improvements in immunosuppressive therapy have been realized. Nonetheless, while one-year transplant success rates have converged considerably, longer term rates continue to remain significantly higher for living-donor kidneys.[71] Absent the organ shortage, however, one would expect to observe a marked decline in the percentage of kidney transplants performed with living donors.

From an overall social cost perspective, living-donor transplants are likely to be substantially more expensive than cadaveric transplants, largely because of the costs imposed on the organ donors.[72] Those transplants place the donor (who is generally a relatively young and healthy individual) at a slight risk of subsequent renal problems or even death. With much greater certainty, however, the operation required to remove the donated kidney (the nephrectomy) is painful and requires a substantial recovery period—as much as four weeks in the hospital with several more weeks (or even months) of restricted activity. Thus, the donor's lost time from work and his or her own pain and suffering add to the cost of the current shortage situation.

We do not dispute that those costs yield substantial social benefits in terms of the recipients' health and productivity. But given the more than adequate supply of cadaveric kidneys that nature (or accidents) provides, they are, to a large extent, unnecessary. An improved cadaveric organ procurement policy could substantially reduce the need for living donors.

Because of the organ shortage, however, reliance on living donors for kidney transplants has increased significantly over the past decade. Table 2-6 documents that increase over the 1988–1998 period. The number of live donors used in renal transplants more than doubled over that ten-year period. During that period, living donors increased from 32 percent of

Table 2-6 Growth in Kidney Donors: Cadaveric versus Living

Donor Type	1988	1989	1990	1991	1992	1993	1994	1995	1996	1997	1998
Cadaveric	3,876	3,810	4,306	4,268	4,276	4,609	4,798	5,001	5,037	5,082	5,327
Increase		-66	496	-38	8	333	189	203	36	45	245
% Increase		-1.7	13	-1	0	8	4	4	1	1	5
Living	1,814	1,903	2,095	2,393	2,536	2,850	3,008	3,347	3,601	3,801	4,016
Increase		89	192	298	143	314	158	339	254	200	215
% Increase		5	10	14	6	12	6	11	8	6	6
Total donors	5,690	5,713	6,401	6,661	6,812	7,459	7,806	8,348	8,638	8,883	9,343
% Living	32	33	33	36	37	38	39	40	42	43	43

Source: www.unos.org/Newsroom/critdata_transplants_ustx.htm.

total donors in 1988 to 43 percent of total donors in 1998; and, today, the number is approaching 50 percent. Thus, the added social costs of such transplants—beyond those warranted by the remaining improvement in transplant success rates—stand as an additional adverse effect of the organ shortage.

Other Consequences. A host of other undesirable consequences of the organ shortage can be identified. For example, the maximum acceptable age of organ donors was increased in recent years—a clear indication that physicians have been forced to make use of less desirable organs in an effort to ease the shortage conditions.[73] Table 2-7 shows the change in the age distribution of cadaveric donors from 1994 to 1998. The number of donor cadavers under fifty years of age has actually declined by 156 over this period, while the number of donor cadavers over fifty years of age increased by 381.

An especially disturbing trend is the increasing use of very young living donors. In 1994 no organs were harvested from living donors under ten years of age. In 1998 twenty-seven living donors under ten years old were reported, including nine under one year of age.[74] While those numbers are small, they point to the increasingly desperate measures resorted to as the shortage of organs grows.

Equally disturbing rumors of various sorts of black-market activities have surfaced in a number of countries, including the United States, as the organ shortage has caused the market value of organs to become increasingly inflated and has driven transplant candidates and illegal brokers to adopt ever more desperate measures.[75] Increasing concerns about the equity of organ allocation mechanisms, including claims of racial discrimination, have also materialized. What appear to be excessive rates of entry into the transplant business have been encouraged by the rents created by an inadequate quantity of organs supplied.[76] And research on cross-species transplants—xenographs—has consumed both scientific effort and research funds in an attempt to resolve the shortage through technological means. All those developments are direct consequences of the ongoing organ shortage. And they all add to the social costs of that shortage.

Table- 2-7 Age Distribution of Donors

Age	1994 Donors	1994 % of Total	1998 Donors	1998 % of Total	Increase 1994–1998	Increase as a % of total change
Over 50	1,157	23	1,538	27	381	55
Under 50	3,928	77	3,772	65	-156	-23
Unreported	15	0	481	8	466	67
Total	5,100	100	5,791	100	691	100

Source: www.unos.org/Newsroom/critdata_transplants_ustx.htm.

Conclusion

A host of technological advances has profoundly influenced the organ transplant business. New, more effective immunosuppressive drugs have been discovered, surgical techniques have improved, better organ preservation methods have been developed, and so on. Those and other technological changes have affected organ supply and demand curves in numerous ways. For instance, on the demand side, transplant success rates have risen, and the set of patients deemed eligible for transplantation has expanded. At the same time, other medical advances—for example, improvements in the treatment of diabetes—have tempered the growth of transplant demand. And, on the supply side, technological change has expanded the potential pool of cadaveric donors by allowing the use of more marginal organs. Despite those important advances, however, the organ shortage has remained as the one constant predominant characteristic of the industry.

Like any market, the organ procurement and transplantation market is a system. Both a supply and demand for transplants and a corresponding supply and demand for transplantable organs exist. All interact simultaneously to yield the outcomes we observe. A ubiquitous characteristic of all systems, whether they are biological, mechanical, electrical, or economic, is that a malfunction in one part of the system will frequently lead to problems in other parts of the system. The organ transplant system is no exception. The various adverse consequences identified above are all symptoms of the failure of organ supply and demand to equilibrate. That is, they are all attributable to the shortage of transplantable organs. If those problems are to be resolved, we must first resolve the underlying cause, which is the organ shortage.

3

Alternative Policy Proposals: A Survey and Comparative Economic Analysis

All systems implemented thus far have a common element: they have all failed.

—David E. Jeffries[1]

For over three decades, medical practitioners, students of medical policy, organ procurement personnel, and, especially, patients suffering organ failure have lamented the shortage of cadaveric organs for transplantation. The concern about the inadequate supply of transplantable organs has spawned a large number of professional articles pointing out the extent and consequences of the failure of current cadaveric organ procurement policies to produce a supply of transplantable organs that meets demand.[2] The growth of the literature on this topic has been paralleled by an explosion of articles in the popular press documenting the shortage and describing the human suffering associated with it, often through the personal stories of individual patients.[3]

Two common themes pervade this literature. First, most authors writing on the subject now tend to agree that the current system of cadaveric organ procurement is woefully inadequate and that some fundamental policy change is in order.[4] Second, the individual articles contained in this literature generally advocate some particular alternative system for harvesting organs and argue that the proposed system would, in all likelihood, be preferable to the present system on some specific grounds—usually the number of organs collected.

The problem with such a piecemeal approach to policy development is that no one has yet considered all the policy options simultaneously or in a logically consistent fashion.[5] Rather, each of these articles advocates some specific proposal and attempts to explain why it would represent an improvement over the current system. Consequently, in reading this literature, we are left with the uncomfortable feeling that something must be done, but we cannot be certain what that something is.

Moreover, as virtually any student of public policy will readily agree, institutions and legal rules exhibit considerable inertia. Once in place, a given policy will tend to endure despite widespread recognition of serious flaws in its operation, and new policies that are clearly superior are generally slow to replace the existing institutional arrangements.[6] Because public policies are changed infrequently, it is imperative that, at this critical juncture when a change in our organ procurement system appears imminent, we explore all the feasible policy options so that the best policy may be selected, not just a policy that is marginally better than the existing one. Rational choice requires that we simultaneously evaluate all potential organ procurement systems to ensure that the policy selected dominates all other policy alternatives.[7]

In this chapter we present and briefly evaluate all the currently proposed organ procurement systems of which we are aware. We explore six such systems, drawn from our review of the extensive literature on the subject. While some of these systems may be seen to be variants on the current, so-called altruistic—or express donation—system (for example, routine request and referral), others represent more fundamental changes to the existing policy (for example, organ markets). Following a brief description of those major policy alternatives, we provide a simple welfare economic analysis of the market versus nonmarket approaches to organ procurement. Using the traditional tools of welfare analysis, we show that the organ market proposal clearly dominates all other alternative policies on social welfare grounds. Finally, because any fundamental policy change invariably affects different parties differently, we also describe who the principal winners and losers are likely to be if the organ market proposal is adopted.

Organ Procurement Policy Alternatives

The literature on organ procurement policy is both large and diffuse. It spans a wide range of disciplines and is housed in a variety of publications.

Medical journals, health policy journals, law reviews, economics journals, public policy and political science journals, ethics and philosophy journals, books, magazines, and newspapers all contain articles on this subject. Moreover, emerging shortly after human organ transplantation first became feasible on a widespread basis, the extensive literature spans at least a three-decade period.[8]

Our review of this literature yields at least six alternative policies pertaining to cadaveric organ procurement.[9] Those policies are not necessarily mutually exclusive. It is possible (indeed, perhaps advisable) to combine two or more of them in forging an ideal public policy for organ procurement.[10] Nonetheless, each policy offers its own unique set of advantages and disadvantages, and each has been advocated independently as a method to improve organ collection rates. Consequently, each should first be evaluated independently on its own merits. Before we can usefully debate combination policies, we must first reach some level of understanding regarding the properties of the individual policies that are to be combined.

Before we discuss those policies, however, it is useful to consider why, on an individual basis, the organs of a potential donor may not be retrieved for use in transplantation. At the most fundamental level, only two reasons exist for organ donation not to occur in specific instances. First, potential donors (or surviving family members) may refuse to donate when asked. Moreover, such refusals to donate may be attributable to either a genuine unwillingness to donate or an inept or ineffective request (or both). And second, the request for donation may simply fail to occur.[11] Such failure to request donation, in turn, can arise from a failure to identify potential donor candidates in a timely fashion or a reluctance to broach the subject of donation with the grieving family. All the various policies discussed below can be seen as attempts to improve organ collection rates by addressing one or the other (or both) of those underlying causes of a failure to donate. In evaluating available policy options, then, it is useful to keep the two potential causes of nondonation in mind.

The alternative procurement systems with which we deal here are: (1) express donation (the current "altruistic" system); (2) presumed consent; (3) conscription (or an organ draft); (4) routine request and required referral; (5) compensation; and (6) a market system. Each of those policy options has received some attention in the published literature on organ procurement. A brief description of each of these alternative systems follows.[12]

Express Donation As noted earlier, our current organ procurement policy is codified in the National Organ Transplant Act of 1984. For our purposes, the most predominant feature of the act is that it makes it a felony to buy or sell human organs for the purpose of transplantation. Various statutes pertaining to organ donation exist at the state level as well. Interestingly, however, most state laws do not explicitly prohibit organ sales.[13]

Importantly, this body of legislation did not create a new public policy toward organ procurement but, rather, served to institutionalize the de facto policy that had been in place since organ transplants first became feasible in the mid-1950s.[14] Organ providers (who, because of practical considerations, are generally the families of critically injured accident victims or those who have died from strokes) are not allowed to receive compensation in exchange for granting permission to remove the organs of their deceased relatives.[15] And organ procurers are not allowed to offer or pay such compensation. Therefore, under the current system, a family's decision to allow such removal must be based entirely on its altruistic desire to supply organs to unknown recipients in need of transplant operations.[16] Historically, the incentive for physicians or other health care professionals who are not directly involved in the transplant business to request donation was also motivated largely by altruism, because no explicit payment was received or profit earned for performing that function.[17] Thus, both the incentive to request (demand) and the incentive to donate (supply) depend, to a large degree, on the altruistic inclinations of the parties involved.

It is important to note that this system of altruistic demand and supply has, for at least three decades, consistently failed to yield an adequate number of organs for transplantation. The number of organs donated annually under this policy has fallen short of the number of organs needed by potential transplant recipients every year for at least the past thirty years.[18] As documented in chapter 2, this chronic condition of undersupply has grown progressively worse in recent years, and waiting lists of potential organ recipients have lengthened commensurately. Expected waiting times are now measured in years rather than months, and thousands of patients die each year because a suitable donor organ cannot be found in time. Consequently, continuing appeals to maintain the current system or to attempt to improve it by making marginal changes (for example, by increased spending on potential donor education) are unconvincing. If the system has not worked in over thirty years of application and repeated modifications, it is unlikely that it can be made to work with only minor changes. Real reform is required.

Presumed Consent. The second policy we consider is presumed consent.[19] This policy differs from the current system in that, instead of actively requesting family members' permission to remove the organs of the deceased, procurement officials may simply presume that there is no objection to such removal. Typically, presumed consent proposals provide that this presumption may be overcome by an affirmative statement to the contrary on the part of the potential donor before death or, perhaps, the surviving family members.[20] In effect, such a policy constitutes a weak reassignment of property rights in the organs of the deceased from the donor or the donor's family or both to the general pool of potential transplant recipients. That reassignment is characterized as weak because it allows the potential donor or his or her family to refuse organ donation (or "opt out") simply by stating an objection.[21] No payment is required to overcome the presumed consent to donate.

The fundamental assumption behind presumed consent is that, in general, people are not strongly opposed to organ removal and, given the opportunity to donate, most would choose to do so. The inadequacy of the current system, then, is seen as being primarily attributable to a pronounced failure to request donations rather than an outright refusal to donate. By removing—or, at least, attenuating—the need to make such a request, it is argued that more organs will be collected than under the current system.

A number of alternative institutional arrangements exist under this policy for "opting out" of the organ donation process. Such arrangements vary across two dimensions. First, they differ in how difficult it is to make one's opposition to organ donation known. And second, they differ in whether to allow family members or the potential donors or both to object to organ removal. For example, individuals may be required to notify in writing some central registry concerning their opposition to having their organs removed at death. Or, alternatively, physicians or others may be required to inform surviving family members of their right to object to organ removal after death. The stringency of the requirements for opting out (for example, whether family members are allowed to object) will obviously influence the ultimate success of this policy in increasing organ donations. Presumably, the more difficult it is to object to donation and the fewer the number of parties allowed to object, the greater will be the resulting collection rates under presumed consent. As a consequence, an inherent tension exists with this and similar policies between individual autonomy (both for the donor and the donor's surviving family members) and the effectiveness of the policy in terms of the number of organs collected. That is, under such policies, improved collection rates come largely at the expense of reduced autonomy for organ donors.

To a large extent, the ultimate effectiveness of any procurement policy will hinge on the willingness of the public to accept that policy. A survey by the United Network for Organ Sharing found that, when individuals were asked whether doctors should be allowed to act on presumed consent, 39 percent said yes, 52 percent said no, and 8 percent were undecided.[22] It would appear then that a policy of presumed consent would not be generally acceptable to the U.S. public.

A number of countries have implemented various versions of presumed consent organ procurement policies, including Austria, Belgium, Finland, France, Greece, Italy, Norway, Spain, and Sweden.[23] Several authors have evaluated the organ collection rates achieved under those policies.[24] Without delving into the specific outcomes, our survey of the literature on presumed consent suggests two important conclusions. First, as expected, the degree of success in terms of observed collection rates is inversely related to the amount of individual autonomy afforded potential organ donors under the terms of the specific policies. That is, the easier it is to "opt out" and the greater the number of parties who are given the opportunity to decline the donation, the lower the resulting collection rate tends to be. Second, and most important, regardless of the amount of autonomy allowed, none of those policies has been able to eliminate completely the organ shortage. According to Jeffries, even Austria, which has the most stringent requirements, continues to experience an organ deficit.[25]

Conscription (or an Organ Draft). A third alternative policy option is conscription. This policy is simply the strongest form of presumed consent. Here, organs of deceased individuals are removed without seeking permission from anyone. In its strongest form, even the donor would have no right to object to organ removal. The property rights to the organs of all deceased individuals are effectively transferred from donors to the pool of potential transplant recipients. In a slightly weaker form, the donor would be allowed to object through some formal channel before death, but the surviving family members would exercise no property rights whatsoever. By completely removing the need to request permission, by making refusal to donate somewhat burdensome, or by restricting the number of parties that have a right to refuse, advocates suggest that this policy could substantially increase organ collection rates.[26]

The conscription proposal appears to have received the least support of any of the alternative policy options in the published literature—and for good reasons. This approach has at least three serious drawbacks.[27] First, it would appear to be very shaky on legal grounds. Specifically, the Fifth Amendment of the U.S. Constitution prohibits the taking of a person's property without compensation.[28] Although the blurry property rights in this area make a definitive conclusion difficult, it would seem, at least on initial inspection, that conscription would not pass legal muster.[29]

Second, as we explain in greater detail below, conscription also exhibits serious deficiencies on economic efficiency grounds. Specifically, where donors and their families have no say in the decision to take the organs of the deceased, it is inevitable that some organs will be removed in situations where either the donor or the surviving family holds strong views in opposition to such an action, perhaps on the basis of religious beliefs. In economic terms, those individuals are the potential organ donors who are located far up and to the right on the organ supply curve. That is, if one were to attempt to purchase the organs of those individuals, the price required to obtain voluntary consent would be extremely high. Under an organ draft, however, those individuals' organs could be taken while the organs of individuals who are far less opposed (that is, exhibit a much lower supply price) could go uncollected. Such indiscriminate collection is economically inefficient, because it does not take into consideration the relative values placed on those organs by the people from whom they are taken.[30]

Third, organ conscription is likely to encounter substantial political opposition and, accordingly, practical resistance. If public acceptance of presumed consent by U.S. citizens is problematic, as the United Network for Organ Sharing survey indicates, conscription is likely to meet with overwhelming objections. Thus, the political feasibility of this policy option is highly doubtful. Moreover, because of its objectionable nature, efforts to implement conscription are likely to encounter opposition on the part of medical practitioners and potential organ donors alike. Specifically, families might insist on maintaining their loved ones on life support until the organs are no longer usable for transplantation. Or they might even refuse to take terminally ill relatives to the hospital if their opposition to organ removal is sufficiently strong. As a result of those and other potential "draft-dodging" strategies, it is possible that the number of organs collected under a policy of conscription could fall below the number currently collected. In addition, the costs of enforcement of this onerous regime could easily exceed the costs experienced under more voluntary alternatives. On both counts—fewer organs and higher costs—this policy proposal could make matters even worse.

Routine Request. Another set of policy options intended to address the problem of failing to request organ donation includes proposals for "routine requests" and "required referrals." Under the first policy, everyone would be required to make his or her wishes known regarding future organ donation at some convenient point in time (for example, at the time driver's licenses are issued or renewed, or at the time income taxes are filed). The individual's expressed preferences would then be recorded with some central registry, or an organ donor card could be provided. In either event, hospital staff would be able to verify readily the stated preference of all potential donors. Then, the organs of all deceased individuals who made premortem commitments for cadaveric organ donation could be routinely removed.

This policy may be expected to improve organ collection rates for three reasons. First, it eliminates the need for the physician or other hospital staff to seek permission from the donor. The potential donor's preferences have already been recorded before death. Second, families of the deceased would not have to be consulted under this policy. The prior statement of the intent of the donor could completely dominate.[31] And third, because the policy requires that an explicit decision regarding organ donation be made by everyone above the age of consent, the concept of organ donation may become more widely known and accepted in society. For all three reasons, it has been argued that donation rates will increase under this policy.

The case for a substantial impact, however, is not supported by the experience with this policy to date. According to Cate, by 1992, forty-six states had enacted some type of routine request policy, generally requiring citizens to indicate their willingness to donate at the time their drivers' licenses are issued or renewed.[32] Thus, we have almost ten years of data to document the effectiveness of this policy. Unfortunately, the data do not appear to indicate a substantial impact on organ supply. And they certainly do not indicate that this policy is capable of eliminating the shortage.

The second policy intended to address directly the failure-to-ask problem—required referral—is obviously focused on the issue of identification of potential cadaveric organ donors at or near the time of death. As noted in chapter 2, this policy requires hospitals to notify their associated organ procurement organizations of all in-hospital deaths. It was recently implemented through regulations issued by the Health Care Financing Administration. According to the transplant surgeons and organ procurement personnel with whom we have spoken, the policy has substantially, if not completely, resolved the problem of failing to identify potential donors. As with required request, however, it has not yet had a significant effect on cadaveric organ collection rates.

Compensation (or Financial Incentives). Unlike the preceding three policy alternatives, all of which focus primarily on alleviating the failure-to-ask problem, the compensation approach addresses the incentive to agree to donation when asked. Here, the families of the deceased are approached by organ procurement personnel regarding permission to remove the organs, just as they are under the current system. Similar appeals to altruism and human kindness can be made. In addition, however, some financial payment or other form of compensation is offered under this system to provide additional encouragement to grant permission to remove the organs of the deceased.[33] It is argued, then, that such payments will lead to an increased rate of organ collection as fewer families decline the request to donate.[34]

Notably, although this policy directly addresses only the incentive-to-donate-when-asked problem, its implementation may serve to alleviate somewhat the failure-to-ask problem as well. Once it becomes widely known that organ donation is compensated, the families of potential organ donors may, themselves, inquire about the opportunity to supply the organs and thereby relieve physicians, nurses, and organ procurement officers from the burden of broaching this sensitive subject. Thus, over time, this policy may serve to increase organ donations through this other channel as well.

Unlike presumed consent (and, a fortiori, conscription), compensation for organ donation appears to have fairly widespread support among the general populace in the United States. When asked whether organ donors should receive some (nonfinancial) compensation for the donation, 52 percent of U.S. respondents to the United Network for Organ Sharing survey answered yes. Only 5 percent of respondents indicated reservations about "potential for problems/abuse" if compensation was used in organ procurement. And, importantly, a mere 2 percent indicated that they considered financial compensation immoral or unethical.[35]

Some (limited) support for this policy alternative also exists within the medical community. Thomas Peters, with the Jacksonville Transplant

Center, first proposed the use of financial incentives in a 1991 article in the *Journal of the American Medical Association*.[36] There, he argued for a (sensitively offered) $1,000 rate of compensation per donor. And later, in 1994, the Council on Ethical and Judicial Affairs of the American Medical Association advocated legislative action that would enable a pilot program to evaluate the impact of financial incentives on donation rates.[37] To date, however, no effective trials have taken place.[38]

Organ Markets. The final policy alternative we consider is that of organ markets.[39] Before delving into the specifics of this alternative, however, we should clarify several issues that have been the source of some fairly widespread misconceptions. First, most proponents of organ markets limit their proposals to cadaveric organs.[40] Indeed, market proponents often cite as a major virtue of the market alternative the declining need for living donors that would follow the expected increase in the number of cadaveric organs supplied as a result of market procurement.[41] In fact, if, as appears likely, the market-clearing prices of cadaveric organs are low, an active market in such organs would be likely to drive out any substantial market in organs from living donors because of the much higher costs of the latter. Thus, while some living-donor transplants (primarily kidneys) would still be performed because of improved success rates, the bulk of them would be from related donors. As a result, an active market in nonrelated living-donor organs may not materialize, even if such a market were not legally proscribed.

Second, those who advocate markets for the acquisition of organs generally do not advocate markets for the distribution of those organs to potential organ recipients.[42] Medical services in general and organ transplants in particular are not now allocated on a strict ability-to-pay basis. Altering the current organ procurement system to make use of market forces to *collect* organs does not require that market forces also be used to allocate them.[43] As a result, the system now used to *allocate* organs among potential transplant recipients could remain unchanged. Of course, in the absence of a shortage, allocation decisions and the so-called tragic choices currently required by the inadequate supply would become much less problematic.

Third, if markets do, in fact, increase the number of organs supplied, as expected, they would in all likelihood reduce, not increase, the overall cost of treatment for patients who suffer from organ failure. For example, dialysis for patients who suffer renal failure is substantially more costly than kidney transplantation.[11] Moreover, the former treatment modality would remain more costly even if transplanted kidneys were purchased rather than donated. As a result, the total expenditures required to treat renal failure would be reduced substantially by the formation of organ markets. Finally, the costs of transplantation are generally paid by third parties, for example, insurance companies or the Health Care Financing Administration, not by transplant patients. Hence, the addition of a price for organs to the bill for transplantation would not exclude low-income patients from receiving transplants.

How, then, would organ markets function? Under a market system, organ suppliers—potential donors or their surviving family members— would be offered a market-determined price (that is, a price that would be allowed to fluctuate with changes in demand and supply) by organ procurement firms for permission to remove the transplantable organs at death. Those firms would then sell the harvested organs to transplant centers that have placed orders with them for needed organs. The centers, in turn, would include the price paid to those firms in the bills for transplant operations, just as all other inputs are currently billed.[45] In a competitive environment, this resale price would equal the price paid to the donor (or donor's family) plus the marginal cost to the firm of collecting and distributing the organs. This additional expense of organ acquisition could be covered by the End Stage Renal Disease Program for kidney transplants and by the recipient's insurance company or other third parties for other organs.[46] Once organs are purchased, the transplant center would be free to allocate them to potential recipients in precisely the same fashion they are allocated today (that is, under the United Network for Organ Sharing guidelines).[47]

As with the previous policies discussed above, any number of potential institutional arrangements could exist under a market system. A futures market could arise in which premortem donors are paid to sign legally binding organ donor cards.[48] Or a spot market could arise in which surviving family members are paid to grant permission to remove transplantable organs.[49] And, as with many other commodities, a spot market and a futures market could, in principle, coexist.[50]

Since markets for organs are poorly understood and often misrepresented, a brief description of how such markets might work in practice seems to be in order. In general, we believe that it is counterproductive to attempt to predict, let alone dictate, the particular institutional arrangements that might arise with the formation of organ markets. Market forces should be allowed maximum freedom to seek out the most efficient methods for resolving the shortage. Nonetheless, it may be useful to outline briefly a potential market arrangement that could conceivably arise. The format for a "feasible organ market" proposed in an article by Hansmann is somewhat typical of market-based organ procurement schemes.[51] Hansmann advocates a market operated primarily, but not necessarily exclusively, by medical insurance companies. Under such a system, policyholders would be given an opportunity to indicate on their premium statements that—in return for a specific reduction in their premium payment—in case of their deaths during the policy period, they would be willing to have their organs harvested for transplantation.[52]

Each insurance company would provide to a national registry a list of policyholders who have consented to organ donation. Upon the death of a potential donor, hospitals would then be required to check this registry. If the patient is enrolled on the registry, notice of the organs that have become available would be disseminated through the national matching network. The prevailing price of any organs transplanted would then be added to transplant costs for the recipient and paid (by third parties) to the donor's insurance company.

It is important to realize that a market system of organ procurement is distinguishable from the policy of compensation discussed above in two important respects.[53] First, under a market system, organ prices would be allowed to fluctuate up or down as supply and demand curves shift. This price flexibility should act to eliminate shortages or surpluses automatically and continuously over time. Under compensation, however, the payment level would likely be set administratively at a fixed level and would not automatically adjust to changes in supply and demand.[54] Consequently, under compensation, surpluses or (more likely) shortages would continue to persist.

Second, under a market system, the organizations (or firms) acquiring the organs for resale to transplant centers would, presumably, operate on a for-profit basis in a competitive environment. As a result, those firms would face powerful market incentives to devise and use the most effective strategies for identifying potential donors and encouraging potential donors and their families to agree to supply the needed organs. For the first time, both the profit carrot and the competition stick would be brought to bear on the organ acquisition process. This incentive structure stands in sharp contrast to the current procurement agencies. As noted earlier, these organizations operate on a nonprofit basis and hold exclusive franchises within their respective collection regions—that is, they are nonprofit monopsonies. Moreover, allowing compensation to organ donors does not alter either of those structural characteristics. Although they may conduct their operations with the best of intentions and work diligently to obtain organs, they are, nevertheless, unlikely to be able to match the performance of for-profit firms in a competitive industry, even if the zero-price constraint is removed (that is, even if compensation is allowed). Thus, while both of these policies allow positive prices, they exhibit important structural differences and are unlikely to yield equal outcomes.

Importantly, with regard to the two fundamental reasons for nonprocurement, the market system is the *only* policy that directly addresses both the failure-to-ask and incentive-to-donate problems. Organ procurement firms would have a financial incentive to seek out potential donors (and, importantly, to conduct the request in an appropriate fashion), and potential organ suppliers would have a financial incentive to agree to organ removal. As a result, it is likely that collection rates would be substantially increased under this policy. In fact, because of the powerful forces of supply and demand, this system should operate to eliminate the organ shortage altogether. Consequently, the remainder of this monograph will focus primarily on the organ market proposal. Before we begin that discussion, however, it is useful to analyze briefly the social welfare implications of the alternative procurement schemes described above.

Social Welfare Analysis

Economists typically conduct comparative policy evaluations by analyzing the impacts of the various policy alternatives on overall social welfare, which is traditionally measured as the sum of consumers' and producers' surpluses.[55] Those surpluses, in turn, are the cumulative excess value received by consumers over and above the expenditures required to purchase a good, and the excess revenues received by producers over and above the returns required to call forth supply, respectively. Graphically, consumers' surplus is generally represented by the area below the demand curve and above the price from zero output up to the quantity purchased. Analogously, producers' surplus is typically given as the area above the supply curve and below the price from zero output to the quantity supplied. Each of those surpluses represents net gains that are realized by each group (consumers and producers) from trade. And their sum, social welfare, measures the total gain to society created by such trade. By comparing the social welfare associated with different policy measures that influence the price and quantity of a good exchanged, we can perform a straightforward comparative evaluation capable of ranking those policies on economic efficiency grounds.

Using those standard tools of welfare economic analysis, it is possible to compare the social welfare implications of the various organ procurement policies described above. For convenience, we treat express donation, presumed consent, and routine request/required referral as a single policy option, because all three of those proposals maintain the legal organ procurement price at zero. In effect, those various modifications to the altruistic system (including the frequently advocated policy of increasing expenditures on education regarding organ donation) are all intended to shift the horizontal (quantity) intercept of the organ supply curve—which represents the number of organs donated at a zero price—to the right. Combining those three policies, then, leaves four basic alternatives to compare: express donation and its variants, conscription, compensation, and organ markets.

Figure 3-1 compares the social welfare associated with the first and the last of those policies—express donation and organ markets. Here, we have

Figure 3-1 Welfare Comparison of Express Donation and Organ Markets

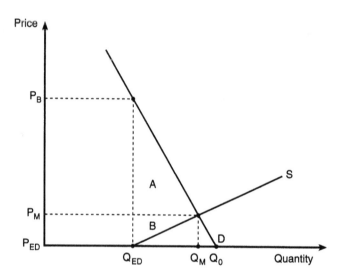

reproduced the organ supply and demand curves shown in chapter 2. As explained there, the legal price under the express donation alternative is zero, and the resulting quantity supplied is Q_{ED}. With organ markets, price rises to P_M and quantity increases to Q_M. A conventional calculation of the resulting levels of consumer and producer surplus under those two alternative policies reveals an unambiguous increase in overall social welfare equal to the sum of areas A and B with adoption of the organ markets proposal.

Two points regarding the magnitude of the increase in social welfare attributable to the formation of organ markets are worthy of note. First, because the organs collected under the current system are not allocated to recipients according to the prices they are willing (and able) to pay, the calculated increase (areas A plus B) will represent a lower bound on the actual increase in social welfare that will be realized by this policy change. This potential understatement of the welfare gains results because some of the additional $Q_M - Q_{ED}$ organs collected under a market system of procurement may well be allocated to recipients whose demand price is above P_B but who, nonetheless, would not have received an organ under the express donation system.[56] Thus, area A + B shows the minimum increase in social welfare attributable to adoption of organ markets.

Second, the magnitude of the increase in welfare is clearly influenced by the price elasticity of organ demand, the price elasticity of organ supply, and the size of the organ shortage. Specifically, the lower the demand elasticity (in absolute value), the higher the supply elasticity, and the greater the shortage, the larger the social welfare gain associated with the organ market proposal will be.[57] Because organ demand elasticity is certain to be low (perhaps zero over the relevant price range), the supply elasticity is expected to be relatively large, and the shortage is also large, the welfare gain is likely to be of a very substantial magnitude.[58] In less technical (and, accordingly, more obvious) terms, a policy that eliminates the organ shortage will be of tremendous value to society.[59]

Next, a comparison of the compensation and organ markets proposals proceeds along similar lines; and, therefore, a separate graph is not required. Assuming that the fixed level of compensation is set above zero but below the market-clearing price, P_M in figure 3-1, analogous, though smaller, areas of increased welfare will be associated with movement to the market system. Moreover, if the level of compensation is set above the market-clearing price, it can easily be shown that social welfare losses will still result as a shortage is transformed into a surplus.

Obviously, the size of the welfare gain achieved by moving from compensation to organ markets will depend largely on how close the level of compensation is set to the market equilibrium price. On the basis of our simple graphical analysis, the two policies achieve identical levels of social welfare if (and only if) the financial incentive is set precisely equal to the market-clearing price. The likelihood of such an outcome, however, appears remote. Also, our graph does not reflect the important differences between these proposals in terms of the market structures (competition versus monopsony) and incentives (for-profit versus not-for-profit) associated with them. Given those differences and the strong likelihood that compensation levels will not be set equal to market equilibrium prices, the organ markets proposal clearly dominates a policy of financial incentives alone on economic efficiency grounds.

Figure 3-2 Welfare Comparison of Conscription and Organ Markets

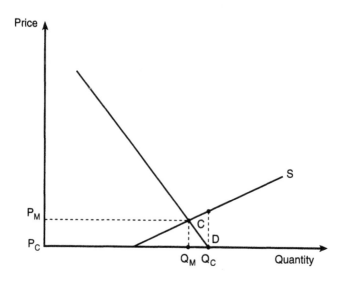

Finally, figure 3-2 provides the social welfare comparison of organ markets and conscription. As before, Q_M and P_M represent the market-determined quantity and price, respectively. With conscription of cadaveric organs, as many organs can be taken as needed to satisfy patients' demand at a zero price. Therefore, under this policy, Q_C (where demand intersects the horizontal axis) organs will be collected and allocated to transplant recipients. Thus, $Q_C - Q_M$ more organs will be harvested under the conscription policy.[60] But, because the patients receiving these organs place a lower value on them than the parties from whom they are taken (that is, because the demand curve falls below the supply curve over the Q_M, Q_C range), a social welfare loss equal to area C is realized under this policy relative to the organ market solution.[61] As before, this area represents the minimum welfare loss associated with conscription, because the Q_C organs are not purchased from voluntary suppliers. As a result, they may be taken from individuals located farther up the supply curve to the right of Q_C. Again, the organ market solution dominates on efficiency grounds.

Thus, the traditional economic criterion for comparative policy evaluation demonstrates, under what we believe are reasonable assumptions, that the organ market proposal is unambiguously superior to the other procurement policies on social welfare grounds. Moreover, while the data required to perform precise calculations of the relevant welfare effects do not exist, the gains that would be realized by allowing organ markets to form would appear to be quite large. The economic case for this policy option is compelling.

Who Wins and Who Loses?

Any major shift in public policy is likely to influence the various affected parties in different ways. Invariably, policy change produces winners and losers, and alteration of cadaveric organ procurement policy is no exception. Numerous interest groups are involved, both directly and indirectly, in organ procurement, allocation, and transplantation; and replacement of the current policy of express donation with a policy that allows cadaveric organ markets to form will affect those groups quite differently. Here, we identify the principal parties that are likely to be influenced directly by such a policy change and briefly describe how they are likely to be affected.

While we discuss several different interest groups here, the interests of some groups seem eminently more worthy of consideration than others. For example, the lives of transplant recipients are at stake. A reasonable person is likely to give saving lives precedence over the psychic discomfort of those who have moral or ethical reservations about a given organ procurement policy. At the same time, a reasonable person is likely to give some weight to other considerations, even when lives are involved. As economists, we are generally reluctant to place one party's interests above another's. Consequently, we describe here the interests of several different groups.

At least five groups would be affected to varying degrees by adoption of the organ market proposal. Those groups are: (1) transplant candidates (both currently and potentially listed); (2) organ donors (both actual and potential) and their families; (3) hospitals, physicians, and other caregivers who supply transplant services; (4) the United Network for Organ Sharing, the Organ Procurement and Transplantation Network, and the organ procurement organizations; and (5) taxpayers and others who finance patient care. Naturally, those groups are not mutually exclusive. For example, organ donors' families, transplant candidates, and caregivers are all taxpayers. In organ procurement, as in most things, individuals tend to operate simultaneously in several spheres. Nonetheless, it can be informative to consider the likely views and incentives in each sphere separately.

Turning to the first interest group, we see that transplant candidates are served best by the policy alternative that yields the largest number of cadaveric organs suitable for transplantation. With a fully adequate supply of cadaveric organs, waiting lists could be trimmed and, over time, eliminated; use of marginal or poorly matched organs could be mini-mized; the need to ask family members to undergo surgery to supply a needed organ could be diminished; and the need to be sustained through dialysis and other difficult but life-preserving treatments could be reduced. All those impacts will greatly improve the health and quality of life of transplant candidates.

Our preceding analysis strongly suggests that, by allowing cadaveric organ prices to rise to equilibrium, market-clearing levels, the organ shortage can be eliminated. While it is theoretically possible that one (indeed, all) of the other policy alternatives could yield as many donors as the market system, such an outcome is extremely unlikely.[62] Unlike the market alternative, none of the other policies embodies the sort of incentive mechanisms that, through the operation of market forces, automatically produces this result. Therefore, the market system of cadaveric organ procurement is likely to best promote the interests of transplant candidates.[63]

Our next interest group, organ donors (and their surviving family members), can benefit from donation in two primary ways. First, they may derive satisfaction from the knowledge that their death, or the death of their family member, has saved the lives and improved the quality of life for others suffering from organ failure. Second, the donor and donor family may benefit in material ways when positive prices are paid for agreeing to donate.[64] And, clearly, this latter benefit is greater the higher the price (or other form of compensation) received.

Compensation and market procurement can both provide both forms of those benefits. All other procurement policy alternatives provide only the former and are, therefore, expected to be less preferred by donors. If we assume that the equilibrium market price is above the compensation level set by the government, then organ donors will tend to favor the market system. On the other hand, if compensation levels exceed the market price, then donors will prefer that policy option. In any event, they will benefit from adoption of one or the other of those proposals because of the positive prices that each entails.

Turning next to the suppliers of transplant services—hospitals, physicians, and so on—we find that it is not altogether clear how their interests play out concerning market versus nonmarket systems of organ procurement. Physicians, in particular, have a variety of (often conflicting) interests—for example, costs, profits, and quality of care. And the weights they place on those various elements of their objective functions may vary greatly across the individual members of the profession. Nonetheless, the American Medical Association, the American Hospital Association, and other professional groups that, ostensibly, represent the interests of their members have been relatively staunch defenders of the altruistic system of organ procurement and have generally expressed opposition to the formation of cadaveric organ markets.[65] Indeed, given the strong political influence of this group, it is probably not an exaggeration to say that the longevity of the policy of express donation is largely, if not completely, attributable to the support of the medical community.

We attempt to provide some insight concerning the likely sources of transplant suppliers' opposition to organ markets in chapter 5. Here, we simply point out that acquisition of a valuable input at a zero price creates economic rents that are likely to be captured by one or more of the participants in the downstream production process, which could include physicians, hospitals, organ procurement organizations, and others. An increase in that input's price to market-clearing levels eliminates such rents and thereby reduces the profits of whatever party (or parties) was (were) receiving them. Transplant suppliers' opposition to organ markets could be motivated (perhaps unconsciously) by this group's perception that, for whatever reasons, they would be net losers from adoption of this policy option. At the same time, however, we also note that the medical community's—particularly physicians'—opposition to this policy shift appears to be waning as those involved directly in patient care grow increasingly frustrated at watching their patients suffer and die unnecessarily because of the lack of a suitable donor organ.

Our fourth primary interest group includes the United Network for Organ Sharing, the Organ Procurement and Transplantation Network, and the organ procurement organizations. As we discuss in chapter 2, those organizations are private, nonprofit institutions that operate under contract with the federal government to procure and allocate transplantable organs under the current system. In effect, those organizations share responsibility for "managing" the shortage and the administrative allocation policies necessitated by it. Here, too, we cannot be completely confident regarding this group's attitude toward organ markets. On purely economic grounds, we would expect them to oppose a major policy shift that eliminates the shortage by introducing for-profit competitive firms into the procurement business. If such a policy were adopted, the organ procurement organizations would lose their monopsony status; and the United Network for Organ Sharing's authority over the allocation process would ultimately become unnecessary as waiting lists gradually disappeared.

But, at the risk of committing blasphemy, economic motivations may not predominate in this particular case. Because these organizations are nonprofit and keenly aware of the tragedies inflicted by the shortage, they may, in fact, be willing to support solutions that promise eventually to eliminate the need for their services or alter the unfavorable market structure within which those services are provided.[66] Therefore, while these organizations may lose economically from the formation of organ markets, we cannot say with complete confidence what their policy position may be.

Finally, the fifth interest group, taxpayers, would unambiguously benefit from adoption of the organ market proposal. As noted earlier, the costs of treating organ failure through transplantation are significantly less than the costs associated with other treatment modalities (for example, dialysis). As a result, the total costs borne by the federal government through programs such as the End Stage Renal Disease Program are likely to fall by a nontrivial amount—probably on the order of several hundred million dollars per year—with adoption of this proposal.[67] Here, however, we encounter the classic public choice problem. The number of people in this group is so large that the financial gain, while substantial in total magnitude, becomes truly trivial on an individual basis. In addition, the members of the group are unlikely to be aware of their interests in this matter, and informing them would be prohibitively expensive. Consequently, while taxpayers would gain by adoption of the organ market proposal, they are, nonetheless, unlikely to present an effective voice at the policy table.

Various other interest groups would also be affected by such a major shift in organ procurement policy. Most obvious, perhaps, would be owners of dialysis clinics. But others, such as health insurance companies, life insurance companies, suppliers of transplant equipment and services, drug companies, and so on would also be affected. The five groups discussed above, however, appear to be the principal stakeholders in this policy debate, and recognition of where their interests lie is, we believe, important.

In summary, three groups would unambiguously benefit from the formation of organ markets—transplant candidates, organ donors, and taxpayers—and two groups would (perhaps) lose—suppliers of transplant services and the organizations responsible for organ procurement and allocation under the current system. Notably, the first groups tend to be heterogeneous, diffuse, and unorganized, while the latter groups are relatively cohesive and extremely well organized. These simple observations may go a long way toward explaining the persistence of the current policy and the shortage it has created.

Conclusion

Those who continue to propose fine-tuning our current organ procurement policy by making only marginal changes to the existing system are clearly on the defensive. The case for meaningful change is too compelling to be resisted much longer. The pertinent question at present is not whether we should have a major policy change, but rather which of the available policy alternatives—or combination of alternatives—should be chosen to replace the current policy.

Finally, in our reading on organ procurement policy, we have observed a propensity on the part of some writers, especially those who publish in medical journals, to adopt a defensive (even hostile) posture regarding changes in the status quo.[68] Their predisposition to support the current policy is often stated in vague and unsupported assertions regarding ethics or the alleged social acceptability of certain policies. Those advocates tend to appeal to the reader's emotion rather than logic, and their work is decidedly nonanalytical. Such an approach makes rational comparisons of alternatives difficult. Our hope is that the above analysis will help to promote a more productive and analytic approach to developing practical strategies for improving organ procurement.

Appendix 3A: An Estimate of the Social Welfare Cost of the Kidney Shortage

In this chapter we present a simple social welfare analysis of the various alternative organ procurement policies. That analysis shows that, relative to the current altruistic system and its variants—all of which hold organ prices at zero—the formation of cadaveric organ markets is likely to increase welfare. Specifically, in figure 3-1 the welfare gain achievable by movement to market-clearing prices is shown as the sum of triangles A and B. And, given what appear to be realistic expectations regarding the empirical characteristics of this market (for example, an inelastic demand, a fairly large shortage, and so on), that sum is, in all likelihood, a relatively large number.

As noted, we do not currently have the ideal data needed to estimate the welfare gains for each transplantable organ. We do, however, have a sufficient amount of information relating to the relevant demand and supply curves for cadaveric kidneys to enable us roughly to approximate that area for this particular organ. The calculation proceeds as follows.

From figure 3-1, assuming linear demand and supply curves, the areas of the two relevant triangles are given by

$$A = \frac{1}{2} (Q_M - Q_{ED})(P_B - P_M) \qquad (3A\text{-}1)$$

and

$$B = \frac{1}{2}(Q_M - Q_{ED})P_M. \qquad\qquad (3A\text{-}2)$$

Summing those areas yields

$$\Delta SW = A + B$$
$$= \frac{1}{2}(Q_M - Q_{ED})P_B, \qquad\qquad (3A\text{-}3)$$

where ΔSW is the change in social welfare achieved by increasing organ donations from Q_{ED} (express donation) to Q_M (the market-clearing level). Therefore, to calculate ΔSW, we need estimates of three parameters—Q_{ED}, Q_M, and P_B.

The first parameter, Q_{ED}, is observable. It is simply the number of kidneys currently collected under the altruistic system, which is given in table 2-1 as 12,955 in 1998. The other two parameters—Q_M and P_B—are not readily observable and, consequently, must be estimated. The first, Q_M, is the quantity of kidneys demanded for transplantation when the price is set at the market-clearing level; and the second, P_B, is the marginal demand price for an additional transplantable kidney at the supply-restricted quantity, Q_{ED}. That is, P_B is the highest price that a potential kidney recipient who did not receive a transplant (because of the shortage) would have been willing to pay to procure the needed organ.

Turning first to P_B, we can only form an educated guess about the maximum price a potential kidney recipient who did not receive a kidney would have been willing to pay for a suitable donor organ. It is certain, however, that this number is quite high. Indeed, the now infamous sham offer of a living-donor kidney on the Internet auction e-Bay generated a reputed maximum bid of $5 million before bidding was suspended. Wanting to err on the conservative side, we assume that $P_B = \$100,000$ for purposes of our calculations.

Next, to estimate Q_M, it is first necessary to estimate P_M, the market-clearing price for cadaveric kidneys. From a survey of college students that we discuss in chapter 6, we estimate a market-clearing price for permission to harvest cadaveric organs at less than $1,000 per donor. According to United Network for Organ Sharing data, on average,

3.2 solid organs are harvested from each cadaveric donor. Because it is unlikely that the market-clearing price will be precisely the same for different organs, it may not be entirely appropriate to simply divide the equilibrium price per donor by the average number of organs harvested to estimate P_M. Nonetheless, this approach does provide a rough approximation for the purpose of our social welfare calculation. Dividing our estimated equilibrium price per donor of $1,000 by the average number of organs harvested from each donor, 3.2, yields our estimate of the market-clearing price for a transplantable kidney of $312.50.

Given our assumed value of P_B = $100,000 and the data provided in table 2-1, we know two points on the cadaveric kidney demand curve, namely, Q_0 = 19,378 at P = 0 and Q_{ED} = 12,955 at P = $100,000. If we assume a linear demand curve, those two points yield a demand function of

$$D = 19,378 - 0.06423P. \tag{3A-4}$$

Substituting P_M = $312.50 into this equation yields Q_M = 19,358 as our estimate of the market-clearing quantity of kidneys.

We now have all three of the parameters needed to calculate ΔSW. From equation (3A-3), above, we have

$$\Delta SW = \frac{1}{2} (19,358 - 12,955) \, 100,000$$
$$= \$320,150,000.$$

That is, the social welfare loss attributable to the current policy that restricts cadaveric organ prices to zero was over $320 million per year in 1998 for kidneys alone.

It is highly likely that this figure underestimates the true welfare cost of the 1998 kidney shortage by a substantial margin. There are at least four reasons to believe that this is the case. First, the $100,000 estimate of marginal demand price is probably much lower than the actual value. The e-Bay auction referred to above certainly suggests that this is the case. A higher value for this price would yield a higher estimate of the welfare loss.

Second, our estimate assumes that the potential recipients who were willing to pay the most for a transplantable kidney (that is, those individuals who have the highest demand prices) received the 12,955 kidney transplants that occurred in 1998. In other words, we assume that those on the transplant waiting list who did not receive kidney transplants and who are therefore those who bear the welfare cost of the shortage were those willing to pay the least for a transplant, that is, those with the lowest demand prices. Since medical criteria, not willingness to pay, are used to distribute organs to potential recipients, this assumption clearly does not hold. The effect of the unrealistic assumption is to reduce our estimate of welfare cost below its true value. Further, given a relatively price-inelastic demand, the amount by which social costs are underestimated by this simplifying assumption is likely to be very large.

Third, as noted in chapter 2, the estimated shortage in 1998 of 6,423 kidneys is apt to underestimate the true shortage. Specifically, our estimate of the shortage is based on the number of patients on the transplant waiting list. As discussed in chapter 2, because of the shortage of available organs, some patients for whom transplantation is a viable and beneficial treatment modality are unlikely to be placed on the transplant waiting list. Obviously, a more accurate measure of the true shortage would yield a larger welfare loss than our estimate.

Fourth, the number of kidneys demanded in 1998 at $P = 0$ was 19,378. Our use of a slope estimate of -0.06423 in calculating Q_M implies that quantity demanded would have fallen to 19,358 if a price of $312.50 per kidney had been charged. In other words, approximately twenty patients who would opt for a kidney transplant when the price of a kidney is zero would opt not to be transplanted when that price is raised to $312.50. The price of $312.50 is a trivial amount relative to the total cost of a kidney transplant, and it is extremely unlikely that the number of patients would fall by that amount. Indeed, it is likely that the number of transplants demanded would not have fallen at all with the imposition of such a small charge. Had we assumed no drop in quantity (which seems very likely) with the imposition of a $312.50 price for transplantable kidneys, our estimate of social cost would have been somewhat higher.

Finally, our estimated welfare loss considers only kidneys. Inclusion of hearts, livers, and other transplantable organs would obviously yield a much higher measure of the welfare cost of the overall shortage of cadaveric organs. Dialysis is a viable alternative to transplantation for kidney patients. But death is the likely alternative to transplantation (at least in the intermediate to long term) for heart and liver patients. As a result, it is likely that the marginal demand prices for hearts and livers at the supply-restricted quantities are much higher than for kidneys. Hence, including other organs in our estimate would dramatically increase our measure of welfare cost, probably by severalfold. Consequently, the total welfare loss attributable to the organ shortage across all solid organs is likely to exceed $1 billion per year.

4

Ethical and Economic Objections to Organ Markets: A Critical Evaluation

People do not resort to arguments as bad as these unless they think arguments are badly needed.

—Janet Radcliffe-Richards[1]

Together, chapters 2 and 3 strongly suggest that organ markets are likely to provide the most promising public policy option for resolving the organ shortage. At the same time, however, a number of concerns—both ethical and economic—have been expressed regarding the moral or ethical acceptability or the economic feasibility of this important policy alternative.[2] Such concerns, in turn, have led a number of commentators either to discount heavily or to rule out completely the market approach.

In this chapter, we critically evaluate the principal arguments that have appeared in the literature on organ markets. In general, we find that those concerns are not well founded, either logically or empirically. In fact, when the arguments that have given rise to those concerns are examined objectively and in any detail, they are readily shown to be either logically specious or based on highly questionable assumptions regarding the underlying parameters of supply and demand functions.

To some extent, the success that such arguments have enjoyed in discouraging even a reasoned consideration of organ markets must be attributed to a certain level of naiveté or outright ignorance concerning the normal operation of market forces. That is, the ability of those arguments to gain any traction whatsoever stems, at least in part, from a lack of economic sophistication among both the proponents and the audiences to which they have been directed.[3] Our purpose here is to expose the rather obvious flaws that those arguments exhibit and, hopefully, thereby to raise the level of debate. We turn first to the literature that has evaluated the ethical properties of the various alternative policy options.

The Ethics of Alternative Organ Procurement Policies

As noted above, the ethical properties of alternative cadaveric organ procurement policies have been the subject of a great deal of discussion. Medical ethicists, philosophers, legal scholars, economists, and medical practitioners, among others, have contributed to an extensive literature addressing the ethics of organ procurement. While considerable disagreement has been expressed in this literature about the ethical merits of each of the policy alternatives discussed above, a consensus now appears to be emerging. A brief survey of this literature is illuminating. It reveals that the range of disagreement is considerably less among those who have extensive training and professional credentials in philosophy and ethics, although a complete consensus does not exist even within that group. The discussion that follows draws largely from the published works of those experts.

The most comprehensive discussion of the ethics of alternative organ procurement policies of which we are aware is that by Childress.[4] Childress posits four "relevant embedded moral principles" that should govern ethical assessments of biomedical issues:

(1) respect for persons, including their autonomous choices and actions;
(2) beneficence, including the obligation to benefit others and to maximize good consequences;
(3) nonmalfeasance, the obligation not to inflict harm; and
(4) justice, the principle of fair and equitable distribution of benefits and burdens.

Using those criteria, Childress concludes that conscription is not ethically acceptable. It violates the principles of autonomy and respect for persons.[5]

Jonsen, however, takes a contrary position, arguing that, while moral autonomy of persons would seem to render conscription ethically unacceptable, this issue is "no longer relevant to the cadaver which has no autonomy and cannot be harmed."[6] But, as Childress points out, Jonsen fails to recognize that people "can be wronged even when they are not harmed."[7] Having one's wishes thwarted after death deprives one of autonomy. Moreover, conscription may also violate the autonomy of surviving family members.

Childress also rejects presumed consent on similar grounds.[8] The requirement that each person actively dissent while living so as to prevent his or her organs from being harvested after death renders presumed consent ethically unacceptable. Failure to dissent may simply reflect a lack of understanding of the mechanism for registering objections or of the course of action when preferences are not explicitly stated. The scope of educational programs required to make presumed consent ethically acceptable imposes such rigorous standards that they are unlikely to be satisfied in any realistic setting.

Quay also argues against the ethical acceptability of presumed consent, stating that "no one, including the state, has any right to make use of a person's cadaver or its parts for research, transplantation, or other purposes, if the deceased has not given his free consent to that use."[9] Quay characterizes a failure of the decedent to consent expressly to donation as a refusal to donate. Hence, presumed consent is seen by Quay as failing the ethical acceptability test because it fails to show sufficient respect for persons.

Evaluated against Childress's moral and ethical principles, routine request–required referral, organ markets, compensation, and the current express donation policy appear morally and ethically acceptable. Administered under circumstances that ensure acceptable standards for informed consent, all those policies are respectful of individual autonomy and freedom of choice, satisfy minimum standards of beneficence and nonmalfeasance, and do not produce obviously unjust distributions of benefits and burdens. Hence, it appears that one can view all four policies as ethically acceptable alternatives.

That characterization, of course, begs the question of relative ethical superiority. No one, to our knowledge, has previously addressed ethical superiority among this group of ethically acceptable options. On the other hand, Caplan claims ethical superiority of routine request over express donation because it is likely to increase organ donation and, therefore, benefit more organ recipients [10] He does not, however, apply the same standard to the remaining policy alternatives.

Also, Mavrodes argues that the transfer of organs through market transactions is superior to the current express donation system because it offers a larger supply of organs for transplantation while still respecting the inherent right of individuals to exercise freedom of choice.[11] A number of nonethicists writing in this field share his view. For example, Hansmann argues that market procurement is superior because more organ recipients benefit and because donors, especially low-income donors, also benefit from the additional income gained through organ sales.[12] Similarly, Schwindt and Vining take the position that organ markets are ethically superior to the current procurement system because the increased supply of organs resulting from the adoption of market procurement would improve equity in the distribution of available transplantable organs, and it would be more equitable to sellers as well because they would be able to reap some of the rewards of their donation.[13]

Childress, while acknowledging the validity of Mavrodes's position, argues:

> It would be ethically and politically unwise to convert the system of donation into a system of sales until these policies have been given a chance to work, in part because transfer by sales would be costly, would probably drive out many donations, and could have serious effects on our conception of personhood and embodiment by promoting commodification.[14]

Childress's assertions that transfer by sales would be costly and that sales are likely to drive out many donations are empirical claims that, we believe, have little merit.[15] On the other hand, the issue whether organ sales, or commodification of organs, is so damaging to our sense of personhood and human dignity as to make markets for organs socially unacceptable has been a topic of considerable philosophical debate.

Perhaps the best, and most complete, explanation of the commodi-fication rationale for organ market prohibition is that offered by Radin. She argues that humans are debased when things like human organs, sexual services, and surrogate motherhood are subjected to the market. She views some things as so closely tied with our sense of self as to be inalienable. Hence, when these things are made alienable, our idea of personhood, integrity, and continuity of self is compromised.[16]

While expressing grave reservations about the use of markets (or even market rhetoric) for human organs, Radin does recognize that mar-ket prohibitions have costs. For example, she notes that a person may feel debased by selling parts of himself or herself or a deceased relative, but he or she may feel even more debased by a prohibition against organ sales. Radin refers to such cases as the "double bind":

> If we think respect for persons warrants prohibiting a mother from
> selling something that is in some sense "inside" her to obtain food for
> her starving children, we do not respect her personhood more by
> forcing her to let them starve.[17]

Radin sees the line between cases in which market transactions should be allowed and those in which markets should be either con-strained or prohibited as hard to draw. On the other hand, she does manage to draw that line for some goods. For example, she favors price controls on housing, because a house is also a home, and some features of "home" are inalienable.

More important for our discussion, she also appears to draw the line with organ sales on the side of market prohibition. She states:

> The act of donating the heart may be one of those distinctively
> human moments of terrible glory in which one gives up a significant
> aspect of oneself so that others may live and flourish.
>
> But now imagine the experience if the grieving parents know that
> the market price of hearts is $50,000. There seems to be a sense that
> the heroic moment now cannot be, either for them to experience or
> for us to observe, in respect and perhaps recognition.[18]

Both Titmuss and Thorne have used the same logic in support of express donation, and prohibition of markets, for human organ procurement.[19]

Frankly, we are continually amazed by such arguments. It certainly could be the case that some persons may feel noble when they donate something of great value (and which is not priced) to someone in need. On the other hand, if a market exists and financial (or other) compensation is available, the sense of self-sacrifice associated with a voluntary uncompensated donation (for those that choose that option) may actually be enhanced since they are now giving up something that has an observable value. In any event, if markets can procure more organs than express donation, as is almost certainly the case, the cost of allowing some persons the satisfaction of a noble act is to deny other persons their very lives.

In a comment on Radin's book, Radzik and Schmidtz offer a very different view on commodification and the double bind. They point out that markets make us rich: they provide us with sufficient wealth that we can afford to devote time to philosophical debates. Radzik and Schmidtz assert:

> [W]hile defenders of markets should admit that some markets are part of the problem, critics should admit in turn that some markets are part of the solution. To commodify some things is to put people in a position where they can afford not to commodify other more important things.[20]

Moreover, Radzik and Schmidtz ask who should be allowed to determine which goods will be subject to market bans and which should be traded in markets. Should we allow Radin to make such decisions or should we allow the individuals themselves to determine what they will trade and what they will not subject to market transactions? In making the point, Radzik and Schmidtz use the example of surrogate mothers. Should the state prohibit a surrogate mother from charging for her services? Or "[s]hould she be allowed to make the call, possibly offending our sensibilities in the process?"[21] Though they are not entirely clear on the point, the answer from Radzik and Schmidtz appears to be that individuals should be allowed to make their own choices, even when others are offended by those choices. This appears to be their position even when we restrict ourselves to the criterion of protecting personhood and human dignity and ignore any efficiency gains that might come from the use of markets: "Letting her make the call is a constituent of her dignity, not just a means to it."[22] To deny someone the right to self-determination is to rob him or her of personhood.

Arrow also takes a view contrary to Radin, though he does think that the issue of commodification is deserving of serious consideration. His point is simple and compelling. He notes that market prohibition requires government action, and government action also adversely affects personhood and human dignity:

> [T]he state and law are overarching systems, just as the market is, and are likely to be just as subversive of the ideals of personhood. Indeed, they may be more so, because the market does provide a sheltered sphere even if stated in commodity terms. Politicizing activities is no greater guarantee of preserving individuation than commodifying them.[23]

Finally, considerable, though not unanimous, agreement exists in the literature that conscription and presumed consent are unethical and that the other four options discussed above are not unethical. At the same time, no substantial agreement exists about the relative ethical superiority of the four remaining acceptable options. In large part, establishing ethical superiority among those procurement policies amounts to splitting some rather fine ethical and philosophical hairs.

The Popular Ethical Arguments against Organ Markets

Less philosophically oriented advocates of maintaining the current organ procurement system—primarily members of the medical community—have argued that it is superior to a market system on the basis of other alleged moral or ethical considerations. While those objections to a market system are not always (or even usually) clearly stated, three major issues appear to dominate most of the discussions in this area.[24] These issues are: a fear of "economic coercion" of the poor; a concern that organ markets would restrict accessibility to transplants by the poor; and an argument that organ markets would have an adverse effect on the incentive of physicians to maintain adequate care for critically ill patients. In the sections that follow, we briefly evaluate the arguments that have been advanced regarding these three issues.[25]

Economic Coercion of the Poor. Several medical ethicists, practitioners, and others have expressed opposition to the use of market forces to increase the number of cadaveric organs supplied on the grounds that families of deceased individuals may be "economically coerced" into agreeing to organ sales that violate their fundamental religious or moral beliefs. The economic coercion argument has at least four major problems. First, it is obviously paternalistic in nature. In effect, the ethicist substitutes his or her own values for those of the individuals involved in the transaction. Market prices provide incentives that induce us to do many things we would not otherwise do, such as going to work, selling a house, or providing goods and services to others. We usually view such payments as a reward for our efforts, not as something that "coerces" us to act. As with any other market exchange, the inducement provided by payment for organs is the (positive) financial gain offered by the organ procurement firm in return for the voluntary agreement to supply. The firm uses no threats or negative sanctions to entice that agreement. As a result, no coercion, in the normal sense of that term, is used under this system.[26] Paying a family to agree to organ donation is no more coercive than paying a coal miner to work in the mine, a professor to teach, or a surgeon to provide medical services. Moreover, the economic coercion argument has the ironic property of leaving the parties one is ostensibly trying to help (by preventing them from being "coerced") worse off (by denying them the opportunity to receive compensation) and thereby exacerbating their poverty.[27]

Second, the economic coercion argument implicitly presumes that the market-clearing price of cadaveric organs will be sufficiently high to provide a financial incentive that overrides fundamental religious or moral beliefs. As noted earlier, however, economic reasoning suggests that the equilibrium price of cadaveric organs is likely to be quite low. That conclusion is based on two observations. First, because of the low collection rates under the current system, excess capacity exists in the market for cadaveric organs. Because we presently collect well under half of the cadaveric organs that potentially could be used in transplant operations, the quantity supplied could easily double or, perhaps, triple before a "capacity constraint" is encountered. In other industries, such a large amount of excess capacity is generally expected to result in a relatively price-elastic supply. That is, a comparatively small increase in price is expected to bring forth a relatively large increase in quantity supplied.

Another reason for expecting a low market price for cadaveric organs is that the opportunity cost of those organs is extremely low. In general, the "next-best alternative use" for cadaveric organs is burial. And because organ removal does not preclude an open-casket funeral, most families are unlikely to place a high value on that use. Consequently, on theoretical grounds, the market-clearing price is likely to be correspondingly low. Moreover, we provide some preliminary empirical evidence that supports this theoretical expectation in chapter 6. A low price, in turn, means that whatever "economic coercion" may be involved in this transaction will be small, and any strongly held beliefs will simply lead to a refusal to sell.

Third, if we are going to base our selection of policy options on the sole criterion of the degree of coercion involved, then we must look at the market system not in isolation but in comparison with our existing system. A market system would create a mechanism for voluntary exchanges at mutually agreeable prices. Under the current system, a physician, nurse, or organ procurement officer must try to coax the family of the deceased to give away for free an asset that could be worth several hundred dollars. Which system involves greater coercion? By favoring the current altruistic system over the market system, the proponent is merely substituting moral or emotional coercion for the alleged "economic coercion" that would accompany a market system.[28]

Finally, those commentators who argue that the market system is economically coercive must accept responsibility for the high price extracted under the current policy to avoid such coercion. In effect, defenders of the present system are trading the lives of others for a policy that they personally prefer because of its reliance on altruism and its (falsely) presumed absence of coercion.

Accessibility by the Poor. A second concern that has helped prevent adoption (or even rational discussion) of a market-based system for organ procurement is the expressed fear that, if organs are purchased from suppliers, only wealthy individuals will be able to afford transplants. The obvious fallacy involved in this argument is that it fails to distinguish between a market for *acquiring* organs and a market for *distributing* organs. Creating a policy that generates a larger supply of organs is analytically separable from creating a policy to allocate that increased supply across income groups. That is, as we noted earlier, use of the market system to procure organs does not require use of the market system to *allocate* them.

An analogy would be our present policy concerning access to food by the poor. We do not stipulate that food prices be zero because of the clear disincentives presented to food producers under such a policy: severe shortages would arise. Instead, we allow market forces to establish equilibrium food prices and then subsidize purchases by low-income individuals. While the food stamp and other agricultural programs are certainly not without flaws, they are, nonetheless, far superior to a policy of free food for the few who could obtain it.

In addition, the accessibility-by-the-poor argument presumes (erroneously, we believe) that market-clearing organ prices would be prohibitively high. Again, both theoretical considerations (chapter 2) and empirical evidence (chapter 6) point to low market equilibrium prices. Moreover, to the extent that discrimination (either racial or income-based) occurs within the current system of organ distribution, it is likely to be reduced or eliminated with an increase in the number of organs supplied. As a result, the poor (as well as the rich) are likely to fare better under a market system of organ procurement.

Premature Termination of Care. The third popular ethical issue pertains to potential incentives for premature termination of care. This problem involves a concern that an organ market might result in unwarranted removal of care from seriously ill patients to obtain transplantable organs to sell. The principal problem with this argument is that, under a market system, the attending physicians would have no direct profit interest in obtaining the organs from the patient.[29] Under such a system, the property rights to the organs of the deceased would be held by the surviving family members.[30] Thus, the donor's family is the only entity that stands to gain financially from the death of the organ supplier. The physician responsible for the patient's care has no more incentive to withhold treatment from a potential organ supplier than from any other patient. The existence of an organ market is, in this sense, similar to a will. It yields benefits to someone from the death of the patient, but no benefits accrue to the physician responsible for the patient's care.

Here, too, comparisons with the current system are warranted. It appears that, as a direct consequence of the organ shortage, the profitability of transplant centers has been artificially enhanced. Such profitability is suggested by the rapid rate of entry by hospitals into the transplant industry during the late 1980s and early 1990s.[31] Consequently, hospitals that have transplant centers may have an adverse incentive to discontinue care for terminally ill patients who are likely candidates for organ donation. We do not believe that this marginal incentive to allow potential organ donors to die is likely to be significant. But the point remains that any potential problem related to premature termination of care is likely to be greater under the current system than it would be with a cadaveric organ market. Shortages invariably bestow artificial value on the affected goods which, in turn, tends to foster black-market activities.

Economic Arguments against Organ Markets

Despite the persuasive case for reliance on the forces of supply and demand to alleviate the cadaveric organ shortage, at least two economic arguments have been raised that could cast doubt on the viability of a market system of organ procurement.[32] First, as noted earlier, it has been argued that the market environment may cause some former altruists to refuse to supply their organs at death, with the result being a discontinuity in the organ supply function and, possibly, a diminution in quantity supplied at positive prices. Second, opponents of a market system claim that such a system may cause the quality of the organs supplied to be lower than that obtained under the current system. We examine each of those economic objections in turn.

Discontinuous Organ Supply. The first economic argument against a market system involves the possibility of a discontinuous organ supply curve at prices above zero. Several commentators have argued that implementing a positive price (compensating either the donor or the donor's family) could reduce the willingness of some individuals to supply their organs at all.[33] In other words, while some people who will not donate at a price of zero might be encouraged to supply organs at a positive price, others who are willing to donate their organs freely would refuse to supply their organs at all if compensation were offered.[34] If the number discouraged from donating exceeds the number encouraged to sell, then the actual quantity of organs made available for transplantation could fall with an increase in price above zero. That is, the supply curve could exhibit an acute discontinuity near the horizontal axis. It would then appear as in figure 4-1, where supply jumps from Q_1 at a zero price to Q_2 at a price of P_2 with the implementation of positive prices.

   If such a discontinuity is present, then an important empirical question is the magnitude of the difference between Q_1 and Q_2. In other words, how much of a reduction in supply is likely to occur with implementation of cadaveric organ sales? In addition, the size of the price elasticity of supply above P_2 becomes an extremely important empirical issue in the event such a discontinuity is present. If supply is relatively flat (that is, elastic) above this point, then any reduction in the quantity supplied in moving from Q_1 to Q_2 may be more than offset by increasing price above P_2 to its equilibrium level. We return to both of these empirical issues in chapter 6.

   Carrying this argument forward, if a significant discontinuity exists in the organ supply function, it is theoretically possible that movement to a market-based system of procurement could result in fewer transplant operations being performed. Such a possibility is depicted in figure 4-2, where the market equilibrium occurs at a price and quantity of P_3 and Q_3, respectively. Altruistic supply, however, yields Q_1 organs for transplantation at a price of zero. Thus, movement from the current altruistic policy

Figure 4-1 Discontinuity in Organ Supply

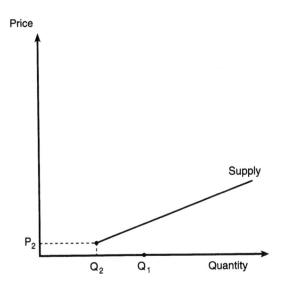

to a market regime apparently leads to a net reduction of $Q_1 - Q_3$ transplantable organs. By this logic, adoption of a market-based procurement policy does not guarantee an increase, and could even lead to a reduction, in the number of cadaveric organs made available for transplantation.

This hypothetical situation, however, deserves considerable skepticism. Two observations indicate that a market system of procurement would be extremely unlikely to create a reduction in the number of transplants. Rather, it appears certain to ensure a substantial increase. First, as we note in chapter 2, organ demand is, in all likelihood, highly price inelastic, meaning that the quantity demanded will not fall much, if at all, in response to an increase in price. And second, the current system yields substantial excess demand. In terms of figure 4-2, this means that the distance between Q_0 and Q_1 is large and that the demand curve is steep above Q_0. Given these observations, then, it is highly unlikely that supply and demand will intersect at a quantity smaller than Q_1. For example, in figure 4-2 it was necessary to draw the demand curve as being relatively price elastic to yield a reduction in the number of organs collected. That is simply not the case for transplantable organs. Demands for these

Figure 4-2 Possibility That an Organ Market Could Yield Fewer
Transplants

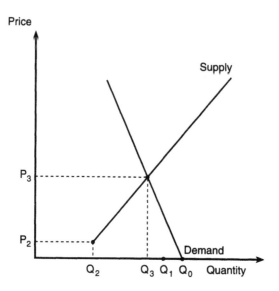

organs are, without question, highly price-inelastic. Thus, on theoretical
grounds, it seems extremely far-fetched to claim that adopting a market-
based system of organ procurement would lead to a net reduction in the
number of organs made available for transplantation as a result of discontinuous supply. Moreover, the empirical evidence pertaining to this issue,
while limited, suggests that such a discontinuity, if present, would be
extremely small in magnitude.[35] Apparently, most people are not morally
offended by the payment of positive prices to organ suppliers; and, importantly, of those who are offended, many will continue to donate or supply
in the presence of such prices. We conclude, therefore, that a market-
based procurement policy will yield more (and, in all likelihood, substantially more) organs than the current altruistic system.

Deterioration of Organ Quality. The second economic argument regarding the use of a market system of procurement involves the potential effect
of compensation on the average quality of the cadaveric organs
harvested.[36] Substituting payments for altruism potentially may reduce

the relative, although not necessarily the absolute, number of organs obtained from comparatively higher income individuals. To the extent that a positive correlation exists between health and income, adopting a market system may decrease the average quality of the organs obtained for transplantation. Thus, some argue for preserving the current altruistic system to maintain cadaveric organ quality. By selecting the current system over a market system, we are seen to be trading quantity for quality. And since organ quality is likely to be an important factor influencing the success of the transplant operation, such a trade-off appears, at first blush, to be potentially justifiable.[37]

Two considerations, however, indicate that the organ quality argument may be incorrect or greatly overstated. First, it is not at all clear that the presumed drop in average quality will materialize. While the forces described above may operate in that direction, other (perhaps, more powerful) forces operate in the opposite direction. As we have pointed out earlier, under the current shortage conditions, surgeons have been tempted, or forced, to make use of marginal or substandard organs.[38] Indeed, the trend toward reliance on more marginal donor organs appears to have accelerated within the past few years. The increased number of organs that would become available under a market system of procurement, however, would enable physicians to exercise greater selectivity in screening acceptable organs for transplantation. Organ quantity and organ quality are not independent variables. Through enhanced screening procedures, an increase in quantity can lead to a corresponding increase in quality.

Second, transplant centers or collection agencies, either government or private firms, are generally able to distinguish organ quality *ex ante* (before the transplant operation). Organs from cadavers cannot be compared to blood collected from living donors who might be infected. For cadaveric organs, the donor pool is the set of accident and stroke victims. Paying for organs will not increase the supply of dead people or alter in any way the distribution or presence of disease or drug use. Consequently, a potential decrement in the average quality of organs *collected* need not lead to a decrement in the average quality of organs *transplanted.* Surgeons performing transplant operations can establish minimum quality standards, and the market price can adjust to yield an adequate supply of organs that meet those standards. We conclude, therefore, that the quality of organs transplanted is likely to improve rather than to deteriorate with the adoption of a market system of procurement.

Conclusion

The above evaluation of the ethical and economic arguments used to justify the current organ procurement policy and to oppose a market-based system reveals fundamental weaknesses with those arguments. They are, virtually without exception, illogical, unfounded, or highly speculative. Others who have subjected those arguments to critical review have been equally unimpressed. For example, Radcliffe-Richards concludes, "Nearly all the objections that appeal to claims about harms caused by organ selling either beg the question, or treat mere possibilities as actual, or fly in the face of positive evidence."[39] And similarly, Dworkin writes, "My conclusion is that, absent other and stronger arguments than those considered, given that both rights and welfare argue in favor of a market for living organ donations, there is no reason not to allow them."[40] Thus, at the present time, there does not appear to be a single persuasive argument that can justify our continued reliance on the current system in lieu of adoption of a more effective procurement policy that relies on market forces.

The obvious questions that emerge at this point, then, are: If the current altruistic system of organ procurement functions so poorly and the arguments used to support it are so obviously flawed, then why is this system so widespread and why has it endured for so long at such great cost? Also, in a related vein, why are hospital and physician professional organizations so adamantly opposed to a policy that relies on market forces to increase the number of cadaveric organs supplied when such a policy appears virtually certain to save numerous lives, reduce suffering, and lower costs? The following chapter provides some potential answers to those questions.

Appendix 4A: The Literature on Blood Sales

The same two economic arguments currently being used to oppose cadaveric organ markets discussed above—discontinuous supply and quality deterioration—were also raised by opponents of blood sales during the 1960s and 1970s.[41] Specifically, several authors argued at that time that allowing commercial blood banks to purchase blood from individuals (that is, to pay donors) would result in discouragement of altruistic donation, thereby reducing the total quantity of blood collected and, more important, a greater incidence of diseased or contaminated blood being used in transfusions, which would result in a higher incidence of serum hepatitis among recipients of blood obtained from paid donors. Thus, it was alleged that commercialization of the blood supply would lead to reduced collections or a decline in quality or both. On the basis of those arguments and a comparative analysis of the British and U.S. experiences, Titmuss and others advocated complete reliance on an altruistic (or donative) system of blood supply.[42] Because both of these claims are largely empirical in nature, it would appear that our experience with blood markets might provide some relevant information that could be useful in evaluating the validity of these same two arguments with respect to organ sales. Accordingly, we turn here to a brief examination of the prior literature pertaining to blood sales. We examine two specific questions relating to that literature for each of the two relevant issues. First, what do the relevant studies show? Was there, in fact, a marked reduction in total collections or a significant deterioration in quality or both when payments were used to motivate supply? And second, is the blood market evidence, whatever it shows, likely to carry over to cadaveric organ sales? That is, to what extent is this evidence relevant to the current debate on organ markets? We turn now to consider each of these questions.

What Does the Evidence Show? Anyone who has conducted empirical research knows that there is no such thing as totally unambiguous, definitive evidence. All empirical studies are subject to qualifications and caveats that render their findings at least somewhat ambiguous. The literature on blood sales is no exception. In fact, it would not appear to be an exaggeration to say that the empirical findings in this area are not capable of reliably supporting any completely definitive conclusions regarding the issues we are considering here.

First, and most informative, with regard to the issue of a discontinuous supply, the blood market evidence appears to provide no indication of a significant reduction in total collections as the result of payments to donors. Upton appears to have conducted the most direct investigation of this issue. In that study a fixed payment of $10 per pint was offered to two separate groups who were already blood donors—one group that had donated on a regular basis and another group that had donated occasionally. The effect of the payment was found to differ markedly between the two groups, with the first group reducing donations and the second group increasing them.[43] As Hansmann noted, while this finding suggests some reduction in supply on the part of those strongly disposed to voluntary donation, it, nonetheless, fails to reject the hypothesis that offering payments to the population in general will result in a substantial increase in the amount of blood collected.[44] Because of the limited structure of the study, it is not possible to observe the effect of the $10 payment on individuals who had not donated at all at a price of zero or the effect of payments greater than $10 on all groups.[45] Moreover, it is worth noting that, today, the American Red Cross and other procurers of blood employ a variety of inducements, both financial and in-kind, to increase collections. This evidence, then, while somewhat equivocal, does not support the claim that commercialization is likely to reduce overall collection rates.[46] That is, the discontinuity of supply (or discouragement of altruism) does not appear to be an empirically significant phenomenon. This conclusion is, perhaps, the most important lesson we can glean from our experience with blood sales.

Second, the blood market evidence pertaining to the quality issue is more ambiguous. As Titmuss and others have emphasized, the incidence of serum hepatitis among recipients of commercial blood has been found to be approximately eleven times greater than that observed among recipients of donated blood.[47] Opponents of blood sales have leapt from this observation to the policy conclusion that payments to donors should be proscribed to ensure a safer blood supply.

A more careful analysis of the economics of purchased versus donated blood by Kessel, however, revealed that the likely cause of the observed quality differential was not the fact that one group of donors was paid while another was not.[48] Rather, Kessel argued first that in the absence of donor screening, payment tended to attract relatively higher risk donors (for example, derelicts, drug addicts, and prisoners) and second that strict limitation of legal liability for contaminated blood effectively removed the market incentive to improve the safety of the blood supplied through implementation of donor-screening procedures. As a result of that legal exemption from liability, the only parties in a position to screen out high-risk donors were indemnified against their failure to do so.[49] In other words, the unusual legal environment within which this market operated created incentives for suppliers to eschew (costly) donor-screening measures that would have ensured higher product quality. Consequently, we cannot conclude that commercial blood is inherently lower quality than donated blood.

Thus, the evidence presented by blood sales is only partially illuminating with respect to the two issues considered here. The literature on this subject provides no indication of a significant reduction in the quantity supplied as a result of payment of positive (but low) prices and thus suggests that discontinuity of supply is not a significant deterrent. And, while some have argued that, empirically, commercialization of the blood supply led to a deterioration in quality, the causal link is rendered ambiguous by the legal rules that have been applied to that market.

Is the Blood Market Evidence Relevant? Whatever one might conclude regarding what, if anything, the blood market evidence shows, that evidence may or may not be relevant to an analysis of the likely performance properties of cadaveric organ markets. Depending on the fundamental similarities and differences between those markets, our experience with purchased blood may or may not carry over to purchased organs. It is useful, therefore, to consider briefly some of the important differences likely to distinguish the two markets. At least three such differences, pertaining primarily to the quality issue, stand out.[50]

First, whereas suppliers of commercial blood typically engage in repeat sales, cadaveric organ suppliers can sell but once. As a result, as Cohen points out, there is no "disproportionality problem" with organ sales.[51] That is, while a supplier of inferior quality blood may taint a disproportionately large share of the overall blood supply, a cadaver's organs can only be harvested once. Thus, the quality issue is unlikely to be as severe with organ markets.

Second, it would appear that quality assurance efforts are more likely to be undertaken and succeed in the case of cadaveric organs. Not only will the organs carry a higher market value per unit than blood, but the opportunity to inspect and test those organs for defects may be greater as they are being removed from the cadaver.[52] Thus, the cost-effectiveness of quality assurance procedures is likely to be greater in the case of purchased organs.

Third and most important, the persistance, severity, and adverse consequences of shortages are far greater in the organ market than in the blood market. While shortages frequently arise in the latter, they tend to be resolved with increased collection efforts and the use of various monetary and nonmonetary incentives to supply, such as assurance programs.[53] In the interim, blood shortages generally result in the postponement of elective surgical procedures. Organ shortages, on the other hand, are continual and long-standing and result in the deaths of thousands of patients each year. Thus, the importance of bringing market forces to bear to resolve those shortages is far greater in the case of organs. Once again, experience from the blood market would not appear to transfer to cadaveric organ markets.

On the basis of the above considerations, we find that our experience with blood purchases provides some limited, but useful, information regarding the issue of a discontinuous supply. On the issue of product quality, however, the blood market evidence is ambiguous and, in all likelihood, irrelevant. In addition, it is of some interest to note that the same economic arguments have been employed to oppose the use of financial incentives to encourage an increase in the quantity supplied in both those markets.

5

The Medical Community's Opposition to Organ Markets: Some Potential Explanations

Based on the data presented herein, it is clear that the "gift of life"
can be financially lucrative to hospitals and OPOs [organ procure-
ment organizations].

—Roger W. Evans[1]

In chapter 3 we survey the principal alternative policy proposals that have been advanced in the literature for resolving, or at least ameliorating, the organ shortage. That survey, along with the analysis presented in chapter 2, suggests the overall superiority of a market-based resolution of this regulatory-induced problem, at least on economic grounds. Simply put, if the shortage is the result of a government-mandated price of zero for cadaveric organs (as it most assuredly is), then that shortage can be eliminated by allowing market forces to increase that price to the market-clearing level. Higher prices will call forth an additional number of organs supplied. With quantity supplied rising to equal quantity demanded, waiting times for patients needing transplants can be minimized and many deaths prevented.

Moreover, our review of the ethics literature on this subject in chapter 4 reveals no logically sound objections to a market-based system of cadaveric organ procurement on either ethical or moral grounds. Indeed, a dispassionate, reasoned analysis that attaches a significant weight to unnecessary loss of life casts a serious ethical shadow over the current altruistic system, because of that system's pronounced failure to collect a larger number of the available organs. The altruistic system, which creates the shortage and its associated suffering and death, has no legitimate claim to the moral high ground.

Nonetheless, despite the obvious and long-standing failure of the existing system to eliminate the shortage and the ability of organ markets to resolve it successfully, to date, the medical community has steadfastly opposed fundamental changes in the way organ procurement efforts are conducted in this country.[2] Specifically, hospital and physician organizations have adamantly opposed the creation of markets for cadaveric organs. Both the American Medical Association and the American Hospital Association have expressed their support of the current system and their opposition to a market-based approach.[3] Three separate transplant associations have passed resolutions that allow for expulsion of any member taking part in organ purchases and sales. One such resolution characterizes a market system as "abhorrent" and "completely morally and ethically irresponsible."[4] Moreover, the medical community's opposition to organ markets is not confined to the United States. A consensus appears to exist on this issue among professional medical associations in all, or virtually all, countries where transplants are performed. As a consequence of that official opposition, medical communities throughout the world have repeatedly called for minor modifications to the current system— more education, directed giving, required request, anything but organ markets—in response to the increasing shortage.

Given the likely superiority of performance of a market-based cadaveric organ procurement system (chapters 2 and 3) and the lack of any sound ethical objections to it (chapter 4), the obvious question that emerges is: Why is the medical community so adamantly opposed to reliance on (indeed, even a reasoned consideration of) the powerful forces of the marketplace to resolve the organ shortage? One possible explanation is offered by Radcliffe-Richards. After evaluating and rejecting the standard set of alleged ethical arguments against organ markets, she suggests that some powerful but unstated emotional revulsion to payment for human body parts, rather than any coherent logical analysis, underlies a widespread refusal to condone a market-based organ procurement system. That implicit emotional reaction, then, leads people to accept, without question, the patently flawed ethical arguments that, supposedly, would justify this predetermined opposition.[5]

While we suspect that this phenomenon may explain, in part, the medical community's observed opposition to organ markets, we do not believe that it is the principal underlying motivation behind that opposition. If some natural, generally shared human instinct underlies the objection to cadaveric organ markets, one would expect opposition to donor payments to be spread throughout the general population, not confined to the medical community. But while some parties have claimed that such widespread opposition is, in fact, present, empirical evidence seems to suggest otherwise. In general, surveys have found that most individuals are not disturbed or morally offended at the prospect of paying organ donors.[6] Indeed, some individuals are offended that, of all the input suppliers involved in the production of organ transplants, the sole entity not paid is the individual whose consent makes the procedure possible— the organ donor. Thus, Radcliffe-Richards's proffered explanation for the observed reliance on clearly specious arguments fails to account for the fact that, for the most part, the strongest and most vocal opposition to organ sales has been concentrated among members of the medical community.[7]

Given that concentration of opposition, the question then becomes: Are there plausible alternative explanations for physicians and the medical community in general opposing the formation of cadaveric organ markets to resolve the shortage? We believe that there are and, not surprisingly, that economics provides at least part of the answer. Specifically, we demonstrate here that, under quite plausible assumptions, the profitability of transplant centers may be reduced by adoption of a market system of procurement, even though such a system eliminates the organ shortage. That is, a straightforward microeconomic analysis shows that payment of positive prices for cadaveric organs can lower profits even as the number of transplants performed expands. Moreover, the economic model supporting this explanation may apply to any of the organizations involved in the supply of transplant-related services—from the organ procurement organizations to the transplant centers.

As explained earlier, acquisition of a valuable input at a zero price creates economic rents that potentially may be captured by any of the agents involved in downstream production activities.[8] Thus, economic, as well as moral, incentives may help to motivate the observed opposition to organ markets among members of the transplant community. In addition, other institutional and historical explanations appear to exist that may contribute to our understanding of this widespread phenomenon. We briefly point to several of these as well.

The Economic Motive

To analyze the potential profit incentive of transplant providers to oppose the formation of organ markets, we develop a simple microeconomic model of the demand for and supply of both transplantable organs and organ transplants.[9] From this model we can compare the provider profits that are likely to occur under two alternative procurement policies—altruistic (zero-price) supply and an organ market in which price is allowed to rise to equilibrate quantities supplied and demanded. Within this model we attempt to incorporate various distinctive features that are either known or widely believed to characterize the relevant functions (for example, a positive quantity of organs supplied at a zero price, an inelastic demand for both transplants and organs, and so on).

Our model is described in terms of a generic input referred to as "organs" and a generic output referred to as "transplants." Application of the model, then, would require specification of a particular transplantable organ, such as kidneys, livers, or hearts. Also, for clarity, we present the analysis in two separate graphs—one of which relates to organs and the other to transplant operations. Because the demand for organs is derived directly from the demand for transplants and the price of organs affects the overall costs of supplying transplants, these two graphs are functionally related to one another.[10] The latter graph—that pertaining to transplants—forms the basis for our theoretical conclusions.

The organ market graph, figure 5-1, depicts the supply and demand curves for transplantable organs that appear in chapter 2. As drawn here, these curves reflect what we believe are the essential empirical realities of this market. Specifically, the curves depict: (1) a supply curve that yields a limited but positive quantity at a zero price and slopes upward beyond

Figure 5-1 The Market for Organs

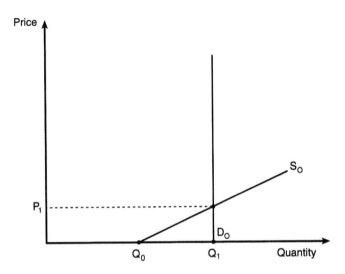

some maximum level of free donations;[11] (2) a demand curve that is extremely price-inelastic (indeed, we have drawn it here with a zero price elasticity); and (3) a significant excess demand, or shortage, at a zero price. These three basic characteristics are consistent with the important empirical features of cadaveric organ markets.[12]

Given the organ supply and demand curves shown in figure 5-1— S_O and D_O, respectively—the market outcome under a policy that restricts price to equal zero is Q_0 organs supplied (or donated). With a quantity of organs demanded equal to Q_1 at this price, there is a resulting shortage equal to $Q_1 - Q_0$ organs per period. This limitation on the quantity supplied (caused by the legal price restriction), then, limits the number of organ transplants that may be performed to Q_0 as well.

If, on the other hand, the price restriction is removed and organ markets are allowed to form, price will rise to P_1 as the number of organs supplied rises to achieve market equilibrium at a quantity of Q_1. This increase in the quantity of organs supplied from Q_0 to Q_1 increases the number of transplant operations that can be performed by an equal amount. At the same time, however, the increase in organ prices from zero

Figure 5-2 The Market for Transplants

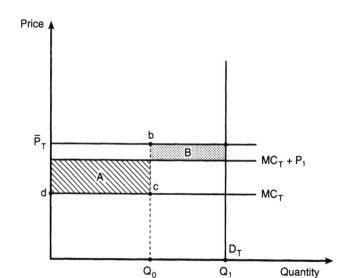

to P_1 also raises the marginal costs of supplying transplants by an amount equal to the equilibrium prices paid for organs.[13]

These impacts of altering organ procurement policies on the suppliers of transplant services are shown in figure 5-2. In this figure, we assume that reimbursement to transplant providers is set by third-party payers—the Health Care Financing Administration or insurance companies—on a fixed fee per procedure basis equal to $\bar{P}_T$.[14] We also assume, for simplicity, that the marginal costs of performing transplants are constant at MC_T. Given the fixed price, $\bar{P}_T$, constant marginal costs, MC_T, and output limited to Q_0 transplants (equal to the Q_0 organs collected), the rectangle $\bar{P}_T bcd$ is the amount contributed to overhead (fixed cost) and profits under the altruistic system of organ procurement (that is, with organ prices fixed at zero).[15]

Now, if organ markets are allowed to form, we will observe two direct impacts on transplant provider profits. First, as organ market prices rise along S_O in figure 5-1, total collections increase from Q_0 to Q_1. This expansion in the number of organs supplied allows transplant suppliers to increase their output by an equal amount—from Q_0 to Q_1 in figure 5-2.

Obviously, this newfound ability to expand output tends to increase the transplant center's profits as long as $\bar{P}_T$ remains above MC_T and fixed costs are unchanged. At the same time, however, the increased prices paid for the organ input push the marginal costs of transplant providers up by an amount equal to these organ prices. Thus, in figure 5-2, the full marginal cost of transplant providers increases to $MC_T + P_1$. This second effect, in turn, tends to reduce profits at the transplant stage.

The net effect on profits of allowing organ markets to form, then, depends on the relative magnitudes of those two opposing effects. The relevant comparison is shown in the two shaded areas marked A and B in figure 5-2, where area A is the reduction in profits attributable to the input price increase and area B is the increase in profits attributable to the output expansion. Thus, transplant provider profits will decrease (increase) if area A is greater than (less than) area B. Those two areas, in turn, depend directly on expected equilibrium organ prices and the amount by which organ collections increase. Assuming, then, that provider profitability is at least one of the considerations influencing the medical community's attitude toward alternative organ procurement policies, this analysis suggests that transplant suppliers will tend to oppose adoption of the organ market proposal to the extent that they believe that market-determined organ prices will be high and that the increase in collections will be low.[16]

Interestingly, those are precisely the expectations that have been expressed in much of the literature in this area. Specifically, critics of the organ market proposal have frequently argued, either implicitly or explicitly, that equilibrium prices would likely be quite high and would raise the overall costs of transplantation[17] and that total organ collections are unlikely to rise appreciably, and may even fall, with the payment of positive prices.[18] The former argument appears to be due to confusion between black-market or supply-restricted demand prices and equilibrium, market-clearing prices; while the latter is due to concerns regarding the discouragement of altruistic donations. The analyses we offer in this monograph—both theoretical and empirical—suggest that these expectations are, in all likelihood, incorrect. Nonetheless, to the extent that these—we believe mistaken—views are widely held by the medical community, the expectation of a negative impact on profits follows. And that expectation, in turn, may influence this group's receptiveness to the organ market proposal.

Also, to the extent that one really believes that market-clearing organ prices will be high and that total collections will not increase significantly, the social welfare gains achieved by movement to a market system of organ procurement will be small or (if collections fall) negative.[19] In this case, then, the profit motive may be consistent with the objective of social welfare maximization. Thus, where these conditions are expected to hold, the medical community's attitude toward organ markets is consistent with maximization of both profits and social welfare. Opposition to organ markets, then, can simultaneously serve the interests of both the bank account and the conscience where a high price and a small impact on donations are anticipated.

Other Sources of Opposition

As economists, we are prone to believe that policy positions are driven largely by the perceived economic self-interest of the affected groups. At the same time, however, we do not rule out other potential motivations or explanations of observed support of or opposition to alternative policy options. Accordingly, we offer here some additional explanations that may contribute to our understanding of the medical community's continued support for the altruistic system of cadaveric organ procurement. At least three such explanations may be identified.[20]

First, as we discuss in chapter 2, the altruistic system emerged naturally during the early days of kidney transplantation as a direct consequence of the exclusive reliance on (well-matched) living related donors. The technological inability to make use of cadaveric donor organs precluded nonrenal transplants, and the absence of modern and affordable dialysis treatments ruled out substantial waiting periods. As a result, the altruistic system of donation was implemented by the transplant community (principally the surgeons performing renal transplants) and, for some time, appeared to work quite well. Indeed, even as cadaveric donor transplants became feasible, the comparatively low levels of effective demand present at that time appear to have been adequately met with altruistic donations alone. Thus, a certain pride of ownership along with an initial experience that supports the idea that the altruistic system can be made to work may, in part, underlie physicians' continued support for that system.

Second, opposition to the organ market alternative appears to have been driven, to a considerable degree, by the early opinions expressed by some of the medical ethicists working in this area. As we discuss in chapter 4, several authors writing in this field during the 1970s and 1980s argued that purchases of cadaveric organs on either a spot or a futures market basis would (or could) violate certain moral or ethical principles. Issues such as economic coercion of the poor, commodification of the human body, and accessibility to transplantation by the poor dominated the thinking on this topic at that time. And physicians, generally lacking extensive training in either ethics or economics as well as the time required for thorough analysis of the relevant issues, relied heavily on the opinions expressed by those ethicists. While the tide of the philosophical debate regarding the moral properties of organ markets appears to have turned in recent years, many practitioners in the medical community continue to be persuaded by the earlier arguments.[21]

Finally, as noted above, both the profitability and social welfare effects of moving from a purely altruistic to a market-based system of cadaveric organ procurement depend crucially on what the price and output effects of such a policy change will be. And, while we are absolutely convinced that market-clearing prices will be low and the impact on collection rates will be large, those are ultimately empirical questions about which we currently have very little data. As a result, while the limited data we do have support our opinions, reasonable people may remain unconvinced that organ markets represent the optimal policy choice. Nonetheless, to the extent that opposition to this policy is founded directly on uncertainty or contrary expectations regarding the empirical effects of adoption of this policy option, those parties should be seeking the data that can reduce that uncertainty and support or reject those expectations. This observation points to the need to implement experimental trials carefully designed to answer those questions.[22]

Conclusion

In earlier chapters we critically examine both the ethical and economic arguments against adoption of a market-based system of cadaveric organ procurement. Without exception, we show those arguments to be, at best, suspect and, at worst, nonsense. At the same time, we show that hospitals and physicians who are the suppliers of organ transplants (and one of the principal groups that have expressed opposition to a market-based system of organ procurement) may have an economic incentive (either real or perceived) to favor the current altruistic system. Thus, provider profits may be expected to be higher under the current system—despite the shortage conditions it creates—than under a market equilibrium that yields increased transplants. That expectation, in turn, is shown to depend on the anticipated price and output effects of adoption of the market-based procurement system. And, interestingly, the same conditions that lead to an expectation of reduced profits also support opposition to organ markets on social welfare grounds. Thus, for those holding what we believe are unrealistic expectations about the empirical impacts of organ markets, there appears to be no inherent conflict between their profits and the public interest.

In addition to the potential economic motivation for this interest group's opposition to organ markets, there exist several possible explanations of a more institutional or historical nature. Specifically, technological constraints affecting the way organ transplants were originally performed, initially favorable experience with altruistic donation, reliance on the early medical ethics literature in this area, and, perhaps, a genuine uncertainty regarding the likely empirical consequences of adoption of the organ market proposal all may have contributed to the official policy position of this group.[23]

Finally, our analysis here is not meant to suggest that physicians and hospitals, or their respective professional organizations, would consciously advocate public policies that increase their profits at the expense of patients' lives. The vast majority of physicians attending transplant candidates appear to experience deep consternation at the plight of their patients. On the other hand, most physicians have neither the time nor the training to analyze fully the economics and ethics of policies their professional organizations support. Most are, quite appropriately, too busy caring for their patients and conducting their own research. More to the point, it seems very likely that a lack of knowledge about the full consequences of the policies they advocate, and not a callous disregard for patients coupled with a single-minded pursuit of personal gain, leads the medical community to advocate express donation over markets. In the presence of uncertainty, it is natural to opt for the policy that is known, even when that policy is not entirely successful. Our hope here is that, by better informing the medical community about the likely economic consequences of this policy, we can persuade those politically influential groups to reconsider their long-standing advocacy of the current organ collection system and their stringent opposition to organ markets.

6

The Question of Supply: Some Preliminary Evidence

[T]here are too few pertinent empirical data. We have based organ-recovery policy on little more than enthusiastic hunches.

—Thomas H. Murray and Stuart J. Youngner[1]

Preceding chapters argue that cadaveric organ markets provide the most promising solution to the shortage of transplantable organs. Because the existing shortage is caused by a public policy that proscribes organ sales, the most straightforward approach to eliminate that shortage is to lift that proscription and thereby allow organ markets to form. The basic appeal of such an approach is that it attacks the underlying cause of the problem instead of merely treating the symptoms.

Obviously, the outcomes achieved under a market solution (that is, the number of cadaveric organs that would be acquired and the market-clearing prices of those organs) depend critically on the demand and supply curves for such organs. As noted earlier, very little uncertainty exists regarding the market demand curve for cadaveric organs. Specifically, the quantity demanded is determined by the number of patients who have been diagnosed as potential transplant recipients, and that number is unlikely to be influenced significantly by the price of cadaveric organs.[2] Consequently, it appears reasonable to assume that cadaveric organ demand curves exhibit zero price elasticity, at least over a fairly wide range of prices.[3]

The same, however, cannot be said about the supply curve of cadaveric organs. At present, no consensus exists regarding how the number of cadaveric organs made available for transplantation is likely to respond to payment of positive prices. While various authors have speculated about the likely slope (or elasticity) and possible shifts in the intercept of the supply curve of cadaveric organs, we are aware of no empirical estimates of those crucial parameters. The reason for this complete absence of evidence, of course, is the fact that observable market transactions for cadaveric human organs have never taken place. As a result, to say that our knowledge of the likely responsiveness of organ supply to the provision of financial incentives (that is, positive prices) is extremely limited is an understatement. While we can offer some educated guesses based on some simple economic reasoning (see chapter 2), we really know very little about this crucially important policy issue.

Moreover, our ignorance of this subject may be largely, if not primarily, responsible for the failure of interested parties to reach a consensus on the design of a more effective organ procurement system. As we show in chapters 3 and 5, the impacts of adoption of organ markets on both social welfare and transplant provider profits depend crucially on the equilibrium prices and outputs that are likely to materialize under that policy. Indeed, much (if not most) of the ongoing debate can be distilled down to an underlying disagreement regarding the equilibrium prices and outputs that would likely be observed under a market system. And those prices and outputs, in turn, depend crucially on the underlying parameters of the supply curve.

In this chapter we report the first empirical evidence of which we are aware on this topic. We admit at the outset that the information we present is highly imperfect. In particular, our data suffer two major shortcomings. First, the data are drawn from a survey instead of from observed market transactions. And second, our sample is not likely to be representative of the population of potential organ suppliers. The first problem is insurmountable in the absence of such transactions. Its resolution, therefore, must await actual market trials. The second problem could be corrected through administration of the survey instrument to a greatly expanded and more randomly drawn sample. While we are able to make some adjustments in an effort to correct for the likely effects of those problems, we can do nothing to ensure unbiased estimates at this point.

As a result, our empirical results should be viewed as preliminary estimates, given this context.

Nonetheless, we believe that some (albeit imperfect) empirical information is better than none, particularly given the gravity of the subject and the crucial importance of supply curve parameters in forging a more effective public policy in this area. Moreover, the empirical results we obtain are such that even a large alteration in the estimates would not affect the resulting policy conclusions. Consequently, we close our apologies here and proceed to describe what we believe to be some interesting, provocative, and very important evidence.

Organ Supply: The Critical Questions

As noted earlier, parties who have opposed the formation of markets for cadaveric organs or the use of financial incentives in general have founded their criticism on both ethical and economic grounds. Our examination of the ethical arguments against organ markets in chapter 4 finds them unconvincing at best and clearly specious at worst.[4] The economic arguments, however, are principally empirical in nature and, to our knowledge, have not been addressed in any but the most superficial fashion. Interestingly, these latter arguments reduce to two fundamental issues, both of which pertain to particular parameters associated with the supply curve of cadaveric organs.

First, if the current so-called altruistic system of organ donation were replaced with a market system or some other system that relies on the use of financial incentives, would a large portion of the population who are now willing to supply either their own organs or the organs of a recently deceased relative at a zero price become unwilling to supply at any (or, at least, any reasonable) positive price? The concern here is that a significant share of the relevant population could be so morally offended by the "commodification" of the human body that, although willing to donate at a zero price, they would withdraw supply from the market altogether at positive prices.

Economically, such behavior would result in a discontinuity or shift in the quantity intercept of the organ supply curve as prices are allowed to rise above zero. In other words, while we are currently able to collect approximately 9,000 cadaveric kidneys at a zero price, we may obtain only, say, 5,000 at a low but positive price. Clearly, such a response is not beyond the realm of possibility and, if present and severe, could actually reverse the intended effect of offering financial incentives—namely, it could potentially cause fewer organs to become available for transplantation as a result of the provision of such incentives.

The second (equally important) empirical issue relating to the supply of cadaveric organs involves the degree of responsiveness of potential organ suppliers to the provision of increasing levels of payment once a positive price is offered. That is, as price is increased from slightly above zero to substantially above zero, what amount of additional supply would likely be forthcoming? Unlike the preceding question, the issue here is the slope or elasticity of the supply curve over a wider range of positive prices. That is, would the provision of increasingly large financial incentives be likely to cause relatively large or relatively small increases in organ "donations"? Clearly, a sufficiently large responsiveness of quantity supplied to price increases could more than offset even a large negative shift in the quantity intercept. Thus, these two issues are interrelated.

Together, these two empirical issues effectively determine the likely success of any policy that relies on financial incentives to resolve the organ shortage. Depending on the answers to those two questions, such a policy may either alleviate or exacerbate that shortage. Moreover, for a given organ demand, those fundamental questions of supply will also determine the equilibrium, market-clearing price of organs under a market system and, thereby, influence the cost-effectiveness of a market-based organ procurement policy.

Figure 6-1 illustrates how crucial the answers to those two questions are. Here, the horizontal axis measures the number of a particular cadaveric organ (say, kidneys) supplied, and the vertical axis measures the price (or some equivalent financial incentive). The curve labeled D is organ demand, which, of course, is derived from the demand for organ transplants (which, in turn, is derived from the demand for health). And the three curves labeled S, S', and S'' are alternative hypothetical organ supply curves that exhibit markedly different intercept shifts and slopes.

Figure 6-1 Equilibrium in an Organ Market: The Question of Supply

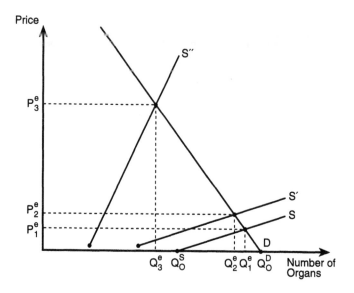

At present, organ prices are set legally at zero. At this price, the number of organs demanded equals $Q^D{}_O$, and the number of organs supplied equals $Q^S{}_O$. The resulting shortage, then, is given by the difference $Q^D{}_O - Q^S{}_O$ per period.

At this time, we are reasonably certain about two empirical facts pertaining to figure 6-1. First, we know that $Q^D{}_O > Q^S{}_O$. That is, at a price of zero, the quantity of cadaveric organs demanded exceeds quantity supplied. Otherwise, no shortage would exist. In fact, as in chapter 2, we can approximate $Q^D{}_O - Q^S{}_O$ from observations on the number of organs demanded and supplied each period at the existing price of zero.

The second empirical fact of which we are certain is that, as noted above, the organ demand curve is likely to be relatively steep (or price-inelastic) over a wide range of prices. This fact is drawn not from empirical observation of organ demand curves over varying positive prices but, rather, from simple economic logic. Specifically, in the absence of close substitutes and the presence of third-party payment, the quantity demanded is likely to be quite unresponsive to price changes over a wide range. That is, the demand curve is extremely price-inelastic, at least at low to moderate prices.[5]

Given those empirical facts, the central question then becomes: How does the supply curve appear at prices above zero? If it appears as S (that is, with no, or a negligible, negative intercept shift in response to the provision of financial incentives and a relatively large overall responsiveness to price changes at prices above zero), then the equilibrium market-clearing quantity will be large (Q^e_1), and equilibrium price will be low (P^e_1). In that event, creation of an organ market will succeed in alleviating the organ shortage in a cost-effective manner. Lives will be saved, suffering will be reduced, and costs will be lowered by movement to a market system for collection of cadaveric organs.

Similarly, if there is a significant negative shift in the horizontal intercept of the supply curve in response to positive prices but a relatively large responsiveness of supply to price changes at prices above zero, the supply curve will appear as S' in the figure. In that event, the market-clearing price and quantity will appear as P^e_2 and Q^e_2. Price will then be higher and quantity lower than occurs with supply curve S. Nonetheless, equilibrium quantity is still substantially greater than Q^s_0, and price is not extraordinarily high.[6] In this case, then, an organ market would still expand the number of organs collected and would eliminate the shortage at costs that remain reasonably low.

If, on the other hand, the organ supply curve appears as S'' (that is, a relatively large negative intercept shift and low responsiveness to price changes), then the resulting equilibrium will occur at quantity Q^e_3 and price P^e_3. Notably, this last equilibrium theoretically could result in a reduction in the number of organs being made available for transplantation in relation to the current number (that is $Q^e_3 < Q^s_0$), although such an outcome is extremely unlikely, given a highly inelastic organ demand. In addition, the high equilibrium price that results in this case impairs the cost-effectiveness of any policy that relies on financial incentives to call forth supply (that is, organ markets or compensation). In this case, movement to a market system of organ procurement could result in increased costs and fewer organs being made available and would thereby cause a reduction in social welfare relative to the current policy.

Clearly, then, the two fundamental questions of supply—the magnitude of the possible intercept shift and the slope of the supply curve—are crucial issues in designing public policies to resolve the organ shortage. Indeed, to a large degree, differences of opinion (often unstated) concerning those two questions are what separate opponents from proponents of a market-based system of procurement once the ethical arguments (and emotional responses) are set aside. We now turn to some preliminary evidence pertaining to those issues.

The Survey Instrument and Sample

To generate the data necessary to investigate the above empirical issues, we designed a written survey and administered it to a broad sample of undergraduate students at Auburn University. Because the individuals in this sample are generally younger and more highly educated than the population of potential organ donors and because age and education have previously been found to influence attitudes toward organ donation, the nonrepresentative nature of our sample is likely to bias our results somewhat. Specifically, because younger, more highly educated people tend to be more receptive to the idea of donating organs (and, perhaps, less opposed to the provision of financial incentives), our sample is likely to produce an upwardly biased estimate of a national organ supply curve.

Two comments regarding this bias, however, are in order. First, the existence and magnitude of the sample-driven bias are uncertain. The evidence concerning the effects of age and education on organ procurement attitudes pertains primarily to donation at a zero price. Those individuals who are most prone to deny the request to donate at a zero price, however, may be relatively more inclined to respond positively to compensation.[7] Also, under current procurement procedures, the person(s) making the decision to donate is (are) typically not the deceased but, rather, the surviving family member(s), whose age and education may be substantially different from the deceased individual from whom the organs are removed. As a result, it is unclear to what degree our results are affected by the particular sample we have selected.

Second, and perhaps more important, given the results we report below, our principal findings would be likely to remain valid even in the presence of a substantial bias. That is, even if we have grossly overestimated the supply curve (or underestimated the supply price) of cadaveric organs, correcting for the bias would not be likely to impair or reverse our basic policy conclusions. In addition, the sheer importance of the subject of this inquiry and the absence of alternative sources of evidence appear to warrant presentation at this time of even preliminary data of this sort. Patients are dying while academicians, practitioners, and policymakers debate what are, at heart, empirical issues in the absence of any data whatsoever. With those considerations in mind, we turn to the survey instrument and resulting sample.

Survey Design and Administration. Our survey, which is reproduced in appendix 6A, consists of twenty questions ranging from whether the respondent has a driver's license and is aware of the voluntary organ donation form on the back of the license to attitudes concerning legalization of the sale of cadaveric organs. Other questions solicit general demographic information as well as responses concerning whether a friend or relative has ever been an organ transplant recipient or donor or whether a friend or relative has ever been on dialysis.

The survey was administered to 392 students enrolled in eight separate courses at Auburn University. Of the 392 surveys distributed, 391 were returned in a usable form. The classes surveyed included two large sections of a university-wide core curriculum course in Political Economy with over 100 students in each, one section of Principles of Macroeconomics, one section of Introduction to Psychology, two sections of Aviation Management, and two sections of Introduction to Communications.

Before distribution of the survey, the following statement was read to each class:

> I want to thank you for your time in completing this survey. Please be deliberate and honest in your answers. These surveys are anonymous and will take approximately 5 to 10 minutes to complete. Be

especially thoughtful in your answers to questions six through eleven. Before you begin, I would like to read you the following short statement. At present, there is a serious shortage of organs for transplantation. Each year about 3,000 people die while waiting for a donor organ. The lives of these people could be prolonged if more donor organs were available. One proposal for increasing the number of donated organs is to offer payments to those who will agree to donate organs. You could, for example, be paid to sign an agreement that, after you die, your organs could be taken for transplantation. Or your family could be paid if they agree to have the organs of a recently deceased relative taken for transplantation. These payments could be in the form of cash, payment of burial expenses, payment of medical expenses, or in many other forms. We want to emphasize that we are only interested in cadaveric organs, that is, those taken from deceased persons. We are not interested in any transactions involving organs taken from living donors. The purpose of this questionnaire is to assess your attitudes about programs that would offer payments for organ donation.

Following this statement, the survey was distributed.

Sample Demographics. The average age of the respondents in our sample was twenty years old, with only eighteen (or less than 5 percent) indicating that they were married and only fourteen (or 3.6 percent) indicating that they had children. The distribution of reported household incomes is shown in table 6-1.

With regard to ethnic backgrounds, the overwhelming majority (349 or 89 percent) of the respondents were white. The remainder of the sample included 29 (or 7 percent) blacks, 4 (or 1 percent) Asians, 1 Hispanic, and 5 who listed "other." Three people surveyed failed to indicate ethnic background. The sample was split almost evenly between males (189 or 49 percent) and females (196 or 51 percent), with 6 respondents failing to indicate sex.

Concerning religious affiliations, 343 respondents (or 88 percent of the sample) indicated that they were members of an organized religion,

Table 6-1 Distribution of Respondents' Annual Household Incomes

Income Responses	Number	Percentage of Total
Less than $10,000	37	9
$10,000 to $30,000	35	9
$30,000 to $50,000	41	10
$50,000 to $80,000	77	20
More than $80,000	127	32
Not sure	70	18
No response	4	1
Total	391	99

while 46 (or 12 percent) indicated no religious affiliation. Of those who were members of an organized religion, the majority (224, or 65 percent) were Protestants.

All 391 respondents had a driver's license at the time of the survey, with 378 (or 97 percent) indicating that they were aware of the voluntary organ donation form on the back of the license. Notably, however, only 92 (or 24 percent) had filled out and signed those forms. Finally, 75 (or 19 percent) of those surveyed indicated that they had a friend or relative who had been an organ transplant recipient or donor, while 90 (or 23 percent) indicated that they had a friend or relative who had been on dialysis.

Supply-Related Questions. The survey contains two sets of questions designed to elicit core information relevant to the supply issues described above—the potential intercept shift that might result from the provision of remuneration to organ donors and the slope of the cadaveric organ supply curve. With regard to the former, three questions were asked concerning respondents' attitudes toward legalization of the sale of cadaveric organs as well as legal conscription of organs.

The first question asked respondents whether they would be offended by the purchase and sale of cadaveric organs, even if such transactions saved lives. Only 47 respondents (or 12 percent of the sample) indicated that they would be offended by such transactions, with 339 (87 percent) indicating that they would not be offended. Five people failed to answer this question.

The second question pertaining to this issue concerned conscription. Here, we asked whether respondents would be offended by a governmental policy that would allow their organs to be removed at death without the donor's explicit permission. The majority (257 or 66 percent) indicated that they would be offended by such a policy, with 134 (or 34 percent) indicating that they would not be offended. Three people failed to answer this question.

For those who responded yes to the conscription question, an additional related question was posed. This follow-up question asked whether the respondent would still be offended by a governmental policy that allows their organs to be removed at death without their explicit permission, even if they could prevent such removal by filing, before their death, a statement denying such permission. As noted in chapter 3, provision of this so-called opting-out mechanism is the fundamental difference between a policy of conscription and a policy of presumed consent. Interestingly, provision of such a mechanism substantially reduced the level of respondents' opposition to such a policy. With this feature added, only 69 (or 27 percent) of the 257 who had previously indicated opposition to such a policy said that they still would be offended, with 188 (or 73 percent) dropping their opposition when the opting-out provision is added.

Finally, three questions were asked concerning the impact of financial incentives on the number of respondents agreeing to donate (or supply) organs. The first of these asked respondents to select from a schedule of payments the smallest amount they would be willing to *accept* to grant permission to have their own organs harvested at death. The second question then asked respondents to select the largest amount they would be willing to *pay* (or have their estate pay) to prevent their organs from being removed, assuming that an organ procurement organization had the right to collect their organs without permission and in the absence of a predeath agreement. The first question appears likely to yield an upward-biased estimate of the supply price, while the second question appears likely to yield a downward-biased estimate of that price.[8]

Hopefully, by framing the question from both sides—the smallest amount they are willing to accept versus the largest amount they are willing to pay—we can bracket the true supply price.

The third question regarding remuneration for organs then asked for the smallest amount the individual would be willing to accept in return for permission to have a relative's organs removed at death. These three questions, along with the preceding questions regarding the potential intercept shift, provide the data required for our empirical analysis of organ supply.

Empirical Results

In this section we report the results of several calculations performed by using our survey results. These calculations are intended to shed some preliminary light on the two principal empirical issues surrounding the question of cadaveric organ supply—the magnitude of the intercept shift and the price responsiveness of supply. Given our analysis of those issues and making reasonable assumptions about the nature of cadaveric organ demand, we are then able to draw certain tentative inferences about the general level of equilibrium, market-clearing prices.

As will become evident, we have chosen to employ a relatively simple, straightforward approach in our analysis of these issues. This choice is motivated primarily by the nature of our data. That is, the above-noted limitations of our data would seem to counsel such an approach in lieu of a more sophisticated econometric analysis. Nonetheless, for comparative purposes, we have also performed some regression-based estimates of supply. These results are reported in appendix 6B. Importantly, these estimates are quite robust and tend to confirm the basic findings that emerge from the simpler approach described here.

Also, throughout the analysis, we intentionally have chosen assumptions that generally tend to result in an overestimation of the supply prices (that is, an underestimation of supply) implied by these data. In this way, we have attempted, to the extent possible, to correct for the biases that are likely to result from both reliance on survey responses (as opposed to actual market transactions) and our nonrepresentative sample. The extent to which such corrective measures are successful, of course, is unknown. We turn now to our calculations.

The Intercept Shift. Several analysts have argued that some individuals who would donate organs without payment would refuse permission to remove organs at death when payments are offered.[9] Presumably, such individuals are so offended by the idea of paying for human organs (the so-called commodification of the human body) that they would withdraw entirely from the organ procurement process if prices or other financial incentives were used to motivate supply. For ease of exposition, we refer to such persons as "market-averse."[10] Of course, the important issue is not whether some persons are market-averse. It is quite likely that some individuals do hold such views. Rather, the important issue is whether the number of those who are market-averse is large relative to the number who would not donate at a zero price but would agree to supply organs if payment were offered. If the latter number exceeds the former number, the payment of positive prices will increase the quantity of organs supplied.

The question in our survey that relates to this issue is the one that asks whether the respondent would be "offended by transactions involving the sale of cadaveric organs." Twelve percent of respondents (forty-seven respondents) indicated that they would be offended by such transactions. Interestingly, however, when these market-offended individuals were then asked the price at which they would sell their organs, only fourteen of these forty-seven respondents (30 percent of those offended by organ sales) indicated that they would not agree to organ harvesting at any price, including zero. Among the other thirty-three market-offended respondents, eighteen (38 percent) listed a price of zero, two left the question blank, and thirteen (28 percent) indicated a positive price at which they would sell.

This information suggests that the negative intercept shift that would accompany the adoption of financial incentives or markets for organ procurement is quite small. Only 12 percent of all respondents were offended by the idea of payments to elicit supply; and of those, only fourteen individuals (30 percent of the 12 percent) indicated that they would not sell at any price in the presence of such payment. Those fourteen respondents comprise less than 4 percent of our total sample.

Hence, to the extent the views expressed by our survey respondents reflect those of the population of potential organ donors, conversion of organ procurement from express donation to organ markets would cause an extremely small supply intercept shift—only about 4 percent.[11]

Importantly, 88 percent of our 391 respondents indicated that they would not find the sale of cadaveric organs offensive. Thus, fully 96 percent of our sample indicated either that they were not offended by organ sales or that they would sell their organs (or agree to donate them) despite being offended by the idea of financial incentives. Thus, the adverse market response to the so-called commodification of the human body does not appear to be a significant phenomenon empirically.

Responsiveness of Supply and Equilibrium Price. Presumably, some individuals who do not currently donate organs when asked—either their own or those of a recently deceased relative—could be induced to agree to donation at a sufficiently high price. This presumption is strongly supported by our survey results, as increasing prices consistently called forth an increasing number of organs supplied. The important policy question, then, is: How high must this price rise to eliminate the current organ shortage? Our survey results can shed light on this crucial issue as well.

To bring our survey results to bear on this question, however, we must first determine the magnitude of the current national organ shortage.[12] Given that shortage, then, we can normalize our sample results to correspond to the national situation by calculating the percentage changes in donations required to eliminate the shortfall and the prices required to call forth those percentage changes. Finally, to operationalize this approach, it is necessary to focus on a single organ. Here, we limit our calculations to kidneys.

In 1997 living donors supplied 3,389 kidneys for transplantation, 8,560 cadaveric kidneys were transplanted, and 3,505 individuals were added to kidney transplant waiting lists. If a sufficient number of cadaveric kidneys were available, the use of living donors would be largely, if not totally, eliminated.[13] Thus, for 1997 an increase of 6,894 cadaveric kidney donations would have been required to replace all living-donor transplants and to provide a sufficient number of kidneys for all those

Table 6-2 Supply Schedule of Organ Donors

Price	Number of Donors
$ 0	138
$ 10	149
$ 25	165
$ 50	183
$ 100	221
$ 500	249
$1,000	299
$5,000	311
Over $5,000	338

who were added to kidney transplant waiting lists. This figure amounts to an 81 percent increase in the availability of cadaveric kidneys.[14] The question, then, is: What sort of price increase would be required to call forth this percentage increase in the quantity of kidneys supplied?

Table 6-2 reports the supply schedule implied by respondents' answers to question 6 of our survey.[15] Here, we have simply added the cumulative number of respondents agreeing to donate their organs at death at each posted price. As this schedule shows, if price were increased from zero to $1,000, the number of donors would increase from 138 to 299. This increase in the number of donors would yield a 117 percent increase in the number of organs procured.

Such an increase would be sufficient to compensate for the resulting negative supply intercept shift and would still more than eliminate the current annual shortage in the number of organs supplied.[16] Hence, these preliminary data suggest that, had market-determined prices been used for organ procurement in 1997, the market-clearing supply price for donors would have been less than $1,000.[17] Because a single cadaveric donor typically yields several transplantable organs, a price of $1,000 per donor would suggest a genuinely trivial price per organ procured, particularly in comparison with the overall cost of a transplant operation.

Finally, at least a portion of this added cost will be partially, if not completely, offset by a reduction in the expenditures currently incurred to induce donors to supply organs with no compensation. It is entirely possible that we are now spending more to elicit "free" donations than it would cost to purchase organs. If that is the case, organ markets would actually lower organ acquisition costs.

Conclusion

Organ transplantation holds the potential to restore the health of many otherwise terminally ill patients substantially. That potential, however, is currently being denied full realization by a chronic and severe shortage of cadaveric organs that are made available for this use. Importantly, that shortage is not due to an inadequate number of deaths that occur under circumstances that would allow transplantation of the deceased individual's organs. Rather, it is directly attributable to a public policy that legally proscribes reliance on market forces to call forth the additional supply that is potentially available. That policy currently results in a collection rate of less than 30 percent of the available supply of cadaveric organs.

That policy, in turn, appears to be founded on two sets of objections to the use of financial incentives or the formation of organ markets. The first involves ethical arguments that, we believe, are generally unfounded. The second set of objections, however, is economic in nature. Those objections pertain to the responsiveness of cadaveric organ supply to the provision of financial incentives. Specifically, such objections focus on a potential negative intercept shift and a projected lack of response on the part of potential organ donors to the formation of organ markets and the provision of financial incentives. To our knowledge, however, empirical evidence concerning those crucial questions regarding organ supply has previously been lacking.

Here, we present some preliminary evidence pertaining to those issues. Significantly, our findings indicate that payment of positive prices has the potential to eliminate completely the organ shortage at very modest levels of remuneration. Specifically, payment of such prices would not cause a substantial shift in the quantity intercept, and positive (but relatively modest) prices would call forth a substantial increase in the number of organs supplied. As a result, the equilibrium, market-clearing price per organ would be quite low—substantially less than $1,000.

As noted, the sample we have used to generate these results is relatively small and nonrepresentative of the relevant population. A larger, more representative sample should obviously be drawn and our results retested. In addition, on the basis of these initial results, carefully designed trials should be conducted in which organ donors' surviving family members are offered direct financial inducements to consent to donation. This two-pronged approach—use of an expanded and more representative sample of survey respondents and actual trials involving payments to donors—appears likely to provide a more solid empirical foundation on which ultimate policy decisions can rest.

Nonetheless, if our findings are even approximately correct, a revision of current public policy that would allow the formation of cadaveric organ markets would create tremendous social welfare gains. Fewer deaths, fewer patients on dialysis, and a significant reduction in overall treatment expenditures would result from such a policy. At least on the basis of these preliminary findings, continuation of the legal proscription on the purchase and sale of cadaveric organs appears to be unwarranted by organ supply considerations.

Appendix 6A: Survey Instrument

Any reference to organs (heart, liver, kidneys, and so on) in this survey strictly refers to organs of deceased individuals.

1. Have you ever had an economics course before?

   ____Yes   At what level?   ____High School
                                                                 ____ Junior College
                                                                 ____College

   ____No

2. What is your major? (biology, sociology, accounting, etc.)

   _____

3. Do you have a driver's license?

   ____Yes   ____No

4. Are you aware of the voluntary organ donation form that is on the back of your license?

____Yes   ____No

5. Have you filled out and signed this form to donate your organs?

____Yes   ____No

6. What is the SMALLEST amount that you would be willing to take from an organ procurement organization to participate in a program that paid people to sign their organ donation form?

____(a) $0–$5	____(e) $100	____(i) over $5,000
____(b) $10	____(f) $500	____(j) I would not be
____(c) $25	____(g) $1,000	interested at
____(d) $50	____(h) $5,000	any price.

7. If, upon your death, an organ procurement organization had the right to take your organ without permission unless you (or your estate) paid to have your organs buried with you, how much is the LARGEST amount that you would be willing to pay (or have your estate pay) to have your organs buried with you?

____(a) over $5,000	____(d) $500	____(g) $25
____(b) $5,000	____(e) $100	____(h) $10
____(c) $1,000	____(f) $50	____(i) $0

8. If an organ procurement organization had a program to allow you to receive remuneration for donating relatives' organs upon their death, what is the SMALLEST amount you would donate for?

____(a) $0	____(d) $50	____(g) $1,000
____(b) $10	____(e) $100	____(h) $5,000
____(c) $25	____(f) $500	____(i) over $5,000

9. Would you be offended by a transaction involving the sale of cadaveric organs (organs from those who are deceased) between individuals (or their estates) if that transaction saved somone's life?

_____Yes, I would be offended by such a transaction.

_____No, I would not be offended by such a transaction.

10. Would you be offended by a policy that allowed the hospital to take your organs, or organs of a deceased relative, without your permission if that taking saved someone's life?

_____Yes, I would be offended by such a policy. (go to question 11)

_____No, I would not be offended by such a policy. (go to question 12)

11. If your answer to question 10 was yes, would you still be offended if you could prevent the organs from being taken by filing a statement denying permission before death?

_____Yes, I would still be offended.

_____No, I would not still be offended.

12. Are you married?

_____Yes   _____No

13. Do you have any children?

_____Yes   _____No

14. Are you self-supporting from an income standpoint?

_____Yes   _____No, I am partially or totally supported by my family.

In which of the following categories would your total annual household income fall?

_____Less than $10,000   _____$50,000 to $80,000

_____$10,000 to $30,000   _____More than $80,000

_____$30,000 to $50,000   _____Not sure

15. What is your age?_____

16. Are you a member of an organized religion?
    ____Yes – To which faith do you belong?

____Baptist	____Methodist
____Catholic	____Presbyterian
____Jewish	____Other

    ____No

17. Of which racial group are you a member?

____Black	____Asian
____White	____Other
____Hispanic	

18. Have you or a friend or relative ever been an organ transplant recipient or donor?
    ____Yes   ____No

19. Have you or a friend or relative ever been on kidney dialysis?
    ____Yes   ____No

20. What is your gender?
    ____Male   ____Female

Appendix 6B: Regression Results

The data in table 6-2 regarding the number of organ donors at various prices have been scaled upward by a factor of 59.81. This scale factor is calculated by multiplying the 8,560 cadaveric kidneys that were transplanted in 1996 by 0.9642, to adjust for those who are "market-averse" and then by dividing that figure by 138. This scale factor normalizes our sample results to represent national figures and yields the data in table 6B-1.

Given these adjusted data, the supply function is specified in log-linear form as:

$$Q_S = \beta_1 + \beta_2 \ln PRICE + \varepsilon_i.$$

Table 6B-1 National Figures for the Supply Schedule of Organ Donors

Price	Number of donors – Q_S
$ 0	8,234
$ 10	8,912
$ 25	9,869
$ 50	10,945
$ 100	13,218
$ 500	14,893
$1,000	17,883
$5,000	18,601

Table 6B-2 Regression Results

Dependent variable = Q_S (number of donors)	
Explanatory variables	
INTERCEPT	6,551.23[a]
	(7.434)
lnPRICE	1,406.05[a]
	(8.195)
Adjusted R^2	0.9043
F value	67.160[a]
N	8

Note: t-statistics in parentheses.
a. Significance level = .01.

This particular functional form was selected on the basis of goodness of fit. Other functional forms were estimated, however, with no substantial alteration in our basic results. Ordinary least squares estimates of the parameters of this equation are reported in table 6B-2.

The overall results appear statistically sound. Both parameter estimates exhibit the expected sign and are significant at the .01 level. Moreover, the explanatory power of this simple model is quite high, with just over 90 percent of the sample variation explained with the price variable alone. Finally, as noted above, our results are quite robust with respect to alternative specifications of the functional form.

Given this estimate of supply, we assumed that the demand curve for kidneys is perfectly inelastic.[18] Also, national figures indicate that an increase of 6,894 cadaveric kidney donations would have been required in 1996 to eliminate the annual shortage completely. The total quantity of kidneys demanded, then, would have been 15,454 (8,560 cadaveric kidney transplants plus 3,389 living-donor transplants plus 3,505 individuals added to the kidney transplant waiting list). Therefore, we have

$$Q_D = 15,454,$$

and

$$Q_S = 6,551.23 + 1,406.05 \ \ln PRICE.$$

In equilibrium, $Q_D = Q_S$. Therefore, the resulting market-clearing price is calculated as being approximately $562 per donor.

Finally, alternative specifications of the supply curve, using different functional forms (linear and log-linear) and combining data from survey questions 6 and 7, were estimated yielding varying equilibrium donor prices. The resulting prices, however, were all within an acceptable range ($135 to $1,509 per donor). Anywhere within this range, the price per organ would clearly be sufficiently low to justify the use of market incentives for organ procurement.

7

Some Thoughts on How Organ Markets Might Operate

The operations for transplantation are sold while the organs (an input) are donated. Either the recipient, the physician, or the hospital receives rents. Both the medical and legal professions have a vested interest in the system.

—R. Larry Reynolds and L. Dwayne Barney[1]

As Adam Smith explained more than 200 years ago, the invisible hand of market forces is capable of amazing organizational achievements. Where they are allowed to operate, these forces bring together, almost as if by magic, productive resources of all sorts to manufacture and transport and bring to market virtually every product for which an effective demand exists. Whether it is bread on the grocer's shelf or a yacht in the harbor, the same underlying forces of supply and demand interact to bring all the necessary inputs together and to ensure that adequate supplies exist at market-clearing prices.[2] Enduring shortages are simply not observed where markets are allowed to function freely.

Given this fact and the evidence—both theoretical and empirical—presented above, it is abundantly clear that resolution of the organ shortage lies in altering existing policies to enable—or, indeed, encourage—cadaveric organ markets to form. An interesting question then becomes: What specific characteristics are such markets likely to exhibit? We believe that it is neither possible nor advisable to delineate or dictate specific features that organ markets should be required to display. Policymakers and would-be advisers—including us—are not omniscient and cannot begin to anticipate the myriad organizational issues that such

markets will have to resolve, nor can we specify in advance the most efficient and effective means for resolving those issues. Rather, market forces
should be allowed to operate as freely as possible, with entrepreneurial
genius given maximum latitude to devise novel, efficient, and currently
unforeseen methods to resolve the organ shortage.

Nonetheless, it is possible to offer some tentative speculations
regarding several of the more prominent features that cadaveric organ
markets are likely to display. Our discussion here is not intended to provide a blueprint for how to organize those markets. Rather, we offer our
opinions primarily to help allay some of the fears that have been expressed
regarding organ markets and to encourage policymakers to refrain from
hampering the market's ability to resolve the shortage by unduly con-
straining the available options.[3] We begin by describing what will *not* be
likely to occur.

What Is and Is Not Being Proposed

Because the issue of markets for human organs is so emotionally charged
and often misunderstood, let us be clear about what advocates of markets
do not propose. They do not propose barkers hawking human organs on
street corners. They do not envision transplant patients, or their agents,
dickering for a heart or liver with families of the recently departed. They
do not generally advocate a market for organs from living donors.[4]
Indeed, markets are seen as a device that could reduce the need for living
donors by increasing the number of cadaveric organs collected.
Proponents of markets do not advocate an auction in which desperate
recipients bid against each other for life-sustaining organs. Indeed, most
market advocates propose using the price system only for organ collection, not for distributing collected organs among potential recipients.

What *is* proposed is a system in which agents of for-profit firms offer
a market-determined price for either premortem or postmortem agree-
ments to allow the firms to collect cadaveric organs for resale to transplant
centers. Any number of potential institutional arrangements could exist
under a market system.[5] For example, insurance companies could enter
the organ procurement market by merging with existing organ

procurement organizations. Then, organ procurement officers who currently negotiate with families of recently deceased individuals could offer those families payment in cash, help with burial expenses, or a number of alternative inducements for the right to remove the needed organs. Such a system would be equivalent to providing the deceased with an *ex post* term life insurance policy with no premium. Alternatively, individuals may be offered a reduction in medical insurance rates in return for a premortem, annually renewable agreement that allows their insurance company to collect and sell their organs in the event that they die during the policy year in a way that makes organ collection feasible. Firms that collect organs would then sell them at market-clearing prices to transplant centers that place orders for needed organs.

Compared with the current policy, markets for organ procurement dramatically change both the incentive of organ procurement personnel to ask for permission to remove organs and the incentive of potential donors to grant that permission when asked. Markets provide tangible rewards, that is, profits, to those who are successful at organ collection. Hence, organ procurement firms would have an incentive to seek out potential donors and to structure requests and payment packages that are most likely to induce a positive response to the request for permission to collect the organs. Further, payment to organ donors provides a direct incentive, in addition to any altruistic inclination they may have, to grant permission.

Organ Markets versus Compensation

Like markets, compensation for organ suppliers provides payment to those who make a premortem commitment to have their organs collected at death or, in its more commonly proposed form, payment to family members when permission to remove organs is given postmortem. Nonetheless, markets for cadaveric organs and compensation for organ suppliers differ in several important respects. Because those differences are often not well understood, a brief discussion of them is in order.

The most important distinctions between markets and compensation concern the way in which prices (compensation) are determined and the types of incentives generated by those prices. Market prices are determined by demand and supply. In organ markets, the prices in question are those paid to organ suppliers (donors) by buyers (organ procurement firms) who, in turn, sell the acquired organs to transplant centers, who may then allocate those organs on the basis of medical need or some other acceptable criterion (for example, degree of tissue match). An important goal of the procurement firm operating in such a market is to make a profit on organ transactions. The opportunity to enhance income by procuring organs provides an incentive for those engaged in procurement to develop strategies (including offering cash, in-kind payments, or a package of both) that are most effective in inducing organ suppliers to agree to having organs removed. Further, since reducing costs can increase profits, organ procurement firms operating in a market regime have an incentive to acquire organs in a cost-efficient manner.

With market procurement, when shortages arise, prices increase. Such increases in price cause the potential profitability from organ procurement to grow. As a result, organ procurement firms offer increased inducements (including higher prices) to organ suppliers. Other things being equal, we would expect those higher prices to induce more organ suppliers to agree to having organs removed and thereby to increase the number of organs supplied. As a consequence, market forces ensure that prices will adjust toward equilibrium (market-clearing) levels and will thus reduce and eventually eliminate shortages. That is precisely how those forces operate in myriad other markets, and no reason exists to expect any different performance in organ markets.

Market forces do not, however, determine the amount paid to organ donors under a compensation policy. As noted earlier, Peters has proposed a $1,000 payment,[6] and others have proposed compensation equal to burial expenses for the donor. Other proposals are similar in that the proposed compensation is set more or less arbitrarily. Further, compensation proposals contain no mechanism that would allow prices to adjust as demand and supply change over time. This means that prices would not move toward equilibrium levels. Consequently, shortages (or surpluses) may persist indefinitely.

In addition, with compensation, those who procure organs do not acquire a property right in the organ and therefore are not the claimants of any profits that might be generated from the efforts required to obtain organs. Compensation, unlike markets, offers little opportunity for those who are in a position to procure organs to increase directly their personal wealth by more effective and efficient procurement efforts. Consequently, those charged with organ procurement simply have less incentive in a compensation system than in a market system to acquire additional organs and to do so in a way that is both effective and cost-efficient. Therefore, to the extent that the existing organ shortage is due to a failure to identify potential donors and to ask for permission to remove organs at death (or to ask for such permission in noneffective ways), compensation does very little to resolve the problem.

In addition to the enhanced incentives that accompany for-profit operations, important market structure differences are associated with the compensation and organ market proposals. Specifically, the former envisions a continuation of the current monopsony structure, where each organ procurement organization holds an exclusive franchise for organ collections within a specified geographic region. Under this system, then, organ procurement organizations face neither the lure of profits nor the threat of competition. Organ markets, however, would accommodate a competitive environment where organ procurement firms are free to enter or exit any geographic area as profit opportunities dictate. Such competition, in turn, will ensure that organ procurement activities are conducted in an efficient and effective manner. The resulting structure-induced differences in performance are likely to be substantial.

In short, organ markets and compensation differ in three important ways. First, with compensation, the form and amount of payment to organ suppliers are largely arbitrary, whereas market prices are allowed to fluctuate with supply and demand so as to eliminate shortages. Second, by introducing the profit incentive, markets provide greater inducements to individuals involved in the procurement process both to acquire more organs and to acquire them in a cost-efficient manner. And third, by altering the market structure associated with procurement activities from monopsony to competition, greater efficiency in organ acquisition will be realized. For all those reasons, the organ market alternative is expected to yield more organs at lower cost than a simple compensation policy that maintains the nonprofit monopsony status of organ procurement organizations.[7]

Markets for Cadaveric versus Living-Donor Organs

To this point, we have focused exclusively on the prospects for markets in cadaveric organs. Indeed, the calculations we have presented—both of the magnitude of the shortage and of the likely height of market-clearing prices—have assumed that cadaveric kidney transplants would completely replace living-donor kidney transplants. That is, we have assumed that the formation of markets in cadaveric organs would completely supplant the use of living-donor organs. At the same time, however, we have recognized that, in general, the arguments we have presented to justify cadaveric organ markets could apply with equal force to markets for living-donor organs (to the extent, of course, that living donation is medically feasible). And, as noted above, there appear to be no ethical or economic considerations that would warrant a legal ban on living-donor organ sales.

Nonetheless, while economic considerations do not justify proscription of living-donor sales, they do suggest that the number of such sales is likely to be relatively small in the presence of well-functioning cadaveric organ markets. The current heavy use of living donors stems from at least two sources. First, living-donor organs appear to be relied on increasingly because of the inability to obtain suitable cadaveric organs within reasonable periods of time as organ waiting lists have grown. That is, to a large extent, it appears that the rising use of living donors is caused largely by the shortage itself. If that shortage can be eliminated, reliance on living donors is likely to decline substantially.

The second reason for the use of living-donor organs, however, appears unlikely to disappear with the formation of cadaveric organ markets. Specifically, while short-term success (one-year graft survival) rates are approximately equal for living and cadaveric donor kidney transplants, the long-term success rates diverge significantly.[8] The data indicate that one-year renal graft survival rates in 1994 were 92.7 percent for living donors and 85.2 percent for cadaveric donors. The five-year graft survival rates, however, were 77.7 percent and 62.5 percent, respectively.[9] Thus, the initial difference is approximately seven percentage points, but that difference more than doubles (to fifteen percentage points) after five years. Consequently, living-donor and cadaveric kidneys are not perfect substitutes.[10] As a result, even if the organ shortage is completely eliminated by cadaveric organ sales, the greater long-term success rates achieved with living donors may result in some continued reliance on such donors.

Economically, the number of living-donor renal transplants performed in the presence of an active market for cadaveric kidneys depends not only on relative success rates—which affect demand—but also on the relative prices of organs obtained from those two alternative sources of supply. Those prices, in turn, depend, *inter alia,* on the underlying costs of supply from those sources. Such costs are clearly much higher for unrelated living-donor organs.[11] For kidneys, a living donor must undergo a nephrectomy to remove the donated organ. That operation is both expensive and painful. It also requires a substantial period of recovery— about a month—during which the donor is unable to work. In addition, while the long-term health risks of giving up a kidney are apparently not substantial, they are also not zero. Cadaveric donors (families of recently deceased individuals), of course, bear none of those costs. As a result, the market-clearing price of living (unrelated) donor organs is likely to exceed the market-clearing price of cadaveric organs by a very wide margin, which further suppresses reliance on the former.

Finally, as cadaveric organ markets begin to equilibrate supply and demand, and as waiting lists shorten and expected waiting times fall, physicians are likely to become somewhat more reluctant to rely on living donors because of the (then unnecessary) risks placed on those healthy individuals. While such risks may be small statistically, the physician's pledge to "do no harm" is obviously violated to some degree by use of living donors' organs.[12] Whether or not organ markets exist, physicians are likely to continue to play an important role in decisions regarding the use of living versus cadaveric donors. Elimination of the shortage, then, would allow physicians to base their recommendations regarding use of living versus cadaveric organs more directly on medical considerations pertaining to the health of both the donor and recipient. In the absence of a shortage, they are likely to become less willing to rely on living donors. Thus, while cadaveric organ markets are unlikely to end reliance on living donors completely, the odds are that the relative use of such donors will decline.

Spot versus Futures Markets

Cadaveric organ markets could feasibly function on either a spot or a futures basis, or both. A spot market would tend to function much like the current system in which potential donors' families are approached at the time of death for permission to remove the organs of recently deceased individuals who meet the criteria for organ donation. As discussed earlier, the principal differences between that system and the current altruistic system are that payments would be allowed to encourage agreement and that profits would be allowed to encourage efficient and effective efforts to obtain such agreement.

A futures market, on the other hand, would tend to operate more like the presumed consent option, except that, instead of presuming consent, organ procurement firms would purchase it. That is, individuals would be paid to enter into contracts for future delivery that would allow the organ procurement firm to remove their organs at death—assuming that death occurs under circumstances that would allow transplantation of those organs.[13] In this case, then, the individual whose organs are to be collected makes the decision to sell, and the surviving family members cannot legally reverse that decision.

As before, no obvious reason exists for policymakers to rule out either of these market alternatives or to favor one over the other. In the absence of any artificial constraints, market forces will encourage use of the option that operates more efficiently. And, of course, it is possible that both spot and futures markets could coexist. Nonetheless, our reading of the literature in this area leads us to suspect that for two reasons spot market transactions are likely to dominate organ sales.

First, the transaction costs associated with a futures market are likely to exceed those associated with a spot market, perhaps by a considerable

Figure 7-1 Spot versus Futures Market Prices

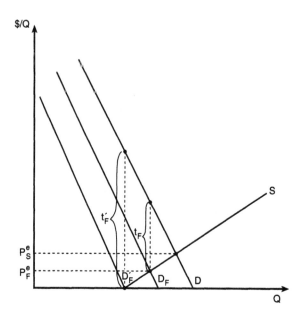

margin.[14] The likelihood of delivery on each futures contract signed will be extremely small, and such delivery will necessarily occur at, perhaps, a very distant point in the future. The contracting parties will not know when the potential donor will die, where the death will occur, and whether death will occur under conditions that will permit transplantation of the donor's organs. Particularly with regard to the third factor, the statistical likelihood that the contracting donor's death will yield transplantable organs is quite small—on the order of 1 percent. As a result, the equilibrium price for those contracts is likely to be extremely low relative to the equilibrium spot market price, because the latter need not be discounted for either time or uncertainty. Moreover, where the spot market price is itself low, a positive equilibrium futures market price may not even exist.

Figure 7-1 shows the relevant comparison. Here, D represents (the spot market) organ demand, and S represents supply. The equilibrium spot market price, then is P^e_S. The impact of substantial transaction costs associated with futures market exchange is to shift the effective demand curve backward and thereby to increase the price paid by the buyer and reduce the price received by the seller, with the difference between the two prices being equal to the per-unit costs of conducting the exchange. If futures market transaction costs exceed spot market transaction costs by an amount equal to t_F, the futures market price will equal $P^e{}_F$; and the two markets will be able to coexist. If, however, futures market transaction costs are equal to or larger than t_F^t, a futures market for cadaveric organs becomes nonviable. Without any prior information on the magnitude of these costs, we cannot say, a priori, which case is likely to hold.[15]

The second reason we expect spot market transactions to dominate futures market contracts for cadaveric organ procurement is more institutional in nature. Specifically, under the current altruistic procurement system, the surviving families of potential organ donors play a central role in determining whether the organs of the deceased will become available for transplantation. In all, or virtually all, cases, permission from the family is sought before the organs are removed.

Importantly, in many cases, such permission is not legally required. As noted earlier, under the Uniform Anatomical Gift Act of 1967, surviving family members need not be consulted where the deceased has executed a valid premortem donor card. Nonetheless, transplant providers not only routinely request the family's permission in such cases, but typically will—contrary to the provisions of the act—override the expressed wishes of the deceased where family members decline permission for organ removal. Moreover, this pronounced tendency to respect family members' wishes apparently transcends the altruistic system employed in the United States. Altman reports that, even in countries that have implemented presumed consent, physicians frequently continue to seek the family's approval before removing donors' organs, even though such consent is not legally required.[16]

There seem to be at least three potential reasons for this observed deference to the surviving family members' preferences. First and, perhaps, most obvious is the legal risk involved. Dead men do not sue; and, in this case, their estates are unlikely to sue, either, because the surviving families have infringed the deceased's prior wishes. Moreover, the injured person is not ascertainable in this situation, since no one knows which patient would have received the uncollected organs. As a result, the provisions of the Uniform Anatomical Gift Act are not enforced, and it is probably safer legally to defer to family members' wishes. Second, having just lost the patient, care providers are understandably reluctant to disappoint or antagonize the family further by taking actions that are against their will. Sincere concern for patients may transfer naturally to concern for their families. And third, a potentially legitimate concern exists that any blatant disregard for family members' preferences could backfire and make future procurement efforts more difficult. Any bad experiences or adverse publicity relating to organ procurement could jeopardize future donors' willingness to participate in the system.

Thus, the medical community's strong inclination to involve family members in the procurement process appears to be a widespread characteristic that any procurement system will need to recognize. And, obviously, spot markets maintain the central role of the surviving family members' wishes, while futures markets do not. Here, again, the spot market solution seems likely to be preferred.

Conclusion

To our knowledge, a free market in cadaveric human organs for transplantation has never been tried. As a result, we have no direct evidence to draw on in forming our expectations regarding how such a market might operate. Partly because of that lack of experience and partly because of the fact that many commentators in this area—physicians, ethicists, attorneys, and so on—are not generally trained in economics, many misconceptions and unwarranted fears have been expressed concerning how such a market might function. The resulting concerns have led many observers to oppose the formation of cadaveric organ markets as a solution to the organ shortage without ever seriously considering the potential for such markets to save lives by successfully resolving that shortage. Hopefully, the discussion we have presented here, speculative though it may be, can help to alleviate some of those concerns and expand the debate to include what is, without question, the most promising policy option—indeed, the only option capable of completely resolving the shortage.

8

Summary and a Call for Action

It seems, however, as if "altruism" is a procurement method preferred by medical professionals and the government, but not the market.

—Christian Williams[1]

In this book we have presented both theoretical arguments and empirical evidence relevant to the issue of the organ shortage and how it may be resolved. We have considered both economic and ethical arguments pertaining to this issue and have reached five significant conclusions.

First, the shortage of cadaveric organs for transplantation has persisted for more than three decades. It is large, growing, and responsible for at least several thousand deaths each year.

Second, the organ shortage is not caused by an insufficient number of potentially transplantable cadaveric organs. Rather, it is the direct result of a public policy that proscribes organ purchases and sales.

Third, economic theory strongly suggests that this shortage can be resolved by changing that policy to allow cadaveric organ markets to form. Such markets would permit cadaveric organ prices to rise and fall as necessary to equilibrate supply and demand and thereby to eliminate the shortage. The social welfare gains achievable through implementation of the organ market proposal appear to be quite substantial, probably exceeding $1 billion per year.

Fourth, ethical objections to cadaveric organ markets appear to be either logically specious or generally unconvincing. Indeed, the alleged moral superiority of any policy that leads to unnecessary deaths must be viewed as inherently suspect. It seems to us indefensible to argue that one group of people should be denied lifesaving transplants simply because another group (which neither supplies nor demands cadaveric organs) prefers altruistic supply over market exchange.

Fifth, initial empirical evidence (though very limited) suggests that adoption of organ markets would completely resolve the shortage at surprisingly low equilibrium prices. It also suggests that the alleged public opposition to such markets has been grossly exaggerated. The medical community, not the public, is opposed to organ markets.

We believe that those findings conclusively demonstrate the desirability, on social welfare grounds, of repealing the ban on cadaveric organ sales contained in the National Organ Transplant Act of 1984. That ban has caused the unnecessary deaths of tens of thousands of patients and prolonged the suffering of many thousands more. And, ironically, it has done this while actually increasing federal and state expenditures on the affected programs. Thus, our current cadaveric organ procurement policy simultaneously kills patients and increases costs. And all of this is done for the high moral purpose of preventing the families of recently deceased accident victims from receiving any payment for their agreement to allow removal of their loved one's organs. It is, frankly, difficult to imagine a crueler, more perverse public system of procurement.

The question, then, is why such a policy continues to endure at the expense of both patients and taxpayers. We believe that at least three factors help to explain the longevity of this policy.

First, the current policy is very much the result of historical accident. It was inherited from a previous era of living-donor-only kidney transplants in which no shortage or, at least, no backlog of patients awaiting a cadaveric donor existed and in which payments to donors were unnecessary or, if necessary, could be made within the family without the need for an intermediary. In that environment, a policy of altruistic (uncompensated) supply made sense. It does not make sense, however, in the current environment of cadaveric organ transplants and chronic shortages. But, once the system was in place, it was simply carried over to the new regime with no real conscious analysis of competing policy alternatives. Thus, simple policy inertia goes a long way toward explaining the longevity of such a system of procurement.

Second, there has been—and, to a large degree, continues to be—a severe lack of information pertaining to the causes, consequences, and potential cures for the organ shortage. Misconceptions related to, *inter alia,* the definition of a shortage, the magnitude of the shortage, the validity of the various ethical oppositions to donor payments, the degree of public opposition to organ markets, and the responsiveness of cadaveric organ supply to positive prices have all contributed to a marked inability of the long-standing debate on organ procurement to achieve any significant convergence of opinions. And to that overall level of ignorance, we must add the inherently emotional nature of the topic. It is very difficult to evaluate opposing arguments in a totally objective light when such fundamental issues are at stake.

And third, as economists, we cannot help but believe that the self-interest of some very influential interest groups has played a significant role in preserving the existing policy. If nothing else, a group's own interest tends to temper its receptiveness to the various competing arguments. Particularly in the presence of uncertainty, it is much easier to be persuaded that a policy option that happens to increase the group's profits is the superior choice.

Given the above factors, then, it is, perhaps, not surprising that the current policy has endured. The question is: Given those factors, what can we do to change the policy? Obviously, we can do nothing about the first of these causes—historical accident—other than simply to point it out. Even that, however, may prove helpful. Once policymakers realize that our present policy is the outcome of historical accident and is not the result of some thorough, objective policy evaluation process, their receptiveness to consider changing that policy may improve. The second cause—lack of information about the cause of organ shortages— however, is addressable, and we hope that the information we have presented here will help to rectify this source of opposition to organ markets. At a minimum, information should help to promote a more logical, less emotional tone for future debate on organ markets.

Finally, the third source of opposition—the self-interest of interest groups—is, perhaps, at least partially open to change. We certainly cannot alter the economic interest that transplant providers and other groups involved in organ procurement and allocation appear to have in maintaining a policy that consistently yields an undersupply of cadaveric organs. We may, however, encourage those groups to temper their opposition and simultaneously encourage policymakers to recognize the conflict of interest those groups have in promoting continued reliance on the current, failed policy.

Notes

Chapter 1: Introduction

1. See Jeffries (1998, 645).

2. See Peters et al. (1996, 2423).

3. See Spieldenner (2000, 1).

4. See ibid., 1.

5. See Barnett, Blair, and Kaserman (1996).

6. See Peters et al. (1996).

7. Implementation of these new provisions subsequently was postponed for one year in response to heated resistance from many of the transplant centers. More recently, congressional action has been proposed to overturn those rules permanently. See Eilperin (2000, A2).

8. The question of who, in fact, holds property rights to the transplantable organs of the deceased is unclear. As Schwindt and Vining (1986) point out, an absence of clearly defined property rights to any valuable asset tends to create problems for resoure allocation decisions.

9. In addition, by allocating organs to the most critically ill patients and by increasing the time between collection and transplantation (by increasing the distance transported), transplant success rates could decline.

10. We describe these actions below.

11. See Jeffries (1998, 632–33).

12. See Evans, Orians, and Ascher (1992) and Gortmaker et al. (1996).

13. See Spieldenner (2000, 1).

14. Jeffries (1998, 645) writes, "The organ transplantation problem is a shortage of available supply, not one of potential supply. . . . The current system is the problem, and it will not be rehabilitated by further tinkering: a new system is needed."

15. More than 6,000 patients died in 1999 while on official organ transplant waiting lists. See Spieldenner (2000, 1).

16. See, for example, Council of the Transplantation Society (1985).

17 See, for example, Peters (1991), Radcliffe-Richards et al. (1998), Amerling (2001), and Finkel (2001).

18. We are not arguing that procurement and allocation are *medically* separable Clearly, the physical characteristics of organs procured will affect the set of patients to which these organs are suitably allocated. Rather, we are simply pointing out that the issue of designing effective procurement policies—the mechanisms through which cadaveric organs can be acquired—is logically distinct from the issue of allocation policies—the mechanisms through which they are allocated.

19. Virtually all principles of economics textbooks treat the subject of shortages. See, for example, Ekelund and Tollison (1994, 98) and Browning and Zupan (1999, 23).

20. While the organ shortage is primarily an economic phenomenon, it carries with it certain issues that are ethical in nature. We consider these as well, but in a much more limited fashion.

21. Our focus is limited to solid (or vascularized) organ—as opposed to tissue— procurement and transplantation. Solid organ procurement and tissue procurement raise somewhat different issues and are, therefore, better treated separately.

22. See Prottas (1985).

23. The most important differences between kidneys and most other transplantable organs are that patients suffering from renal failure have an alternative long-term treatment—dialysis—available to them and that living donors can be used to supply kidneys. Those differences influence the shape and location of the demand curve for kidneys relative to other organs but do not alter our analysis in any fundamental way.

24. To date, the only open, organized organ markets that have come into existence have involved living donors, although some black-market activity in cadaveric organs has been reported. See Altman (1994), Williams (1994), and Finkel (2001). The obvious reason for this is the relative ease of arranging a transaction between a living donor and the recipient. A market for transplantable cadaveric organs has never, to our knowledge, been organized.

Chapter 2: The Organ Shortage

This chapter draws, in part, from Blair and Kaserman (1991).

1. See Cate (1994, 86).

2. For a discussion of the history of policies and funding of transplants, see Rettig (1989).

3. See Pub. L. 98-507, October 19, 1984, 98 Stat. 2339 (Title 42, Sec. 273 et seq.). This law proscribes payments either to living donors or to families of cadaveric donors. We provide a more detailed discussion of this act below.

4. See Denise (1985).

5. In some cases, a death that could have yielded transplantable organs is not recorded as a potential donor, because the attending physician fails to take the actions necessary to preserve the organs adequately. For example, if the blood pressure of the deceased is allowed to drop below a certain level, the organs will be damaged and will be unsuitable for use in transplantation. It is not known how many potential donors are lost from this cause.

6. The medical community's insistence that, despite legislation to the contrary, family members' permission be obtained appears to be grounded on several considerations, which we discuss later in this monograph. It also persists, no doubt, because of a lack of enforcement of the 1967 act's provisions. To our knowledge, no one has ever been prosecuted under this act for failing to remove organs of a deceased individual.

7. We have been informed that, where a donor card has been executed and is located, surviving family members generally tend to consent to organ removal. They rarely override the donor's wishes where those wishes are known. It is also the case, however, that, in many instances, donor cards are not present or are not located. See Cate (1994, 81–82).

8. For example, it has been found that a brief period of time (around twenty minutes) needs to separate the act of informing the family of their loss and requesting organ donations. This separation between the notification of death and the request for donation is apparently needed for family members to assimilate and accept the fact that their relative has died.

9. In one of these cases, the physician, having just informed the family that their relative had died, asked, "You don't want to give away any of his parts, do you?"

10. For various reasons, a number of organs are collected but do not get transplanted. These organs may exhibit physical flaws that are discovered when they are removed from the cadaver, they may be damaged during removal or transport, and so on.

11. A more detailed discussion of this topic may be found in Cate (1994) and Douglass (1996). This section draws from those two sources.

12. See the *Uniform Anatomical Gift Act of 1968,* 8A U.L.A. 63 91993 (superseded by the *Uniform Anatomical Gift Act of 1987*).

13. *The Uniform Anatomical Gift Act* 2(h), 8A U.L.A. 34, provides, "An anatomical gift that is not revoked by the donor before death is irrevocable and does not require the consent or concurrence of any person after the donor's death." See Cate (1994, 72).

14. See the *National Organ Transplant Act,* Pub. L. No. 98-507, 98 Stat. 2339 (codified as amended in scattered sections of 42 U.S.C.).

15. In one incident it was reported that a wealthy sheik from Saudi Arabia had made a $1 million donation to a transplant center's research program and had immediately received a cadaveric kidney transplant.

16. Oversight authorities of the federal government regarding organ allocation issues have expanded over time since the National Organ Transplant Act was first adopted. See Cate (1994, 76–79).

17. See ibid.

18. The Organ Procurement and Transplantation Network and the organizations that participate in it also receive funding from user fees—specifically, patient registration fees and charges to transplant centers for costs incurred in supplying organs to them.

19. Transplant physicians determine whether a given patient is approved to be listed as a transplant candidate.

20. Some organ procurement organizations were in existence as early as 1968, well before passage of the National Organ Transplant Act. See Cate (1994, 77).

21. The transplant centers, in turn, are reimbursed for these expenses under the End State Renal Disease Program.

22. To approach these families, the organ procurement organizations must first be notified by the hospital of the potential donor's death. Recent legislation requires such referrals for all hospital deaths.

23. The monopsony status of the organ procurement organizations within their collection regions is not ironclad. Individual hospitals can, with approval from the Health Care Financing Administration, switch from one organization to another. Such switching, however, is apparently very rare.

24. See 42 U.S.C. 274e(a) (1994).

25. See ibid., 274e(c)(2).

26. These regulations require each hospital to use a "designated requestor" to meet with family members to discuss organ donation. This person must be either provided or approved by the organ procurement organization.

27. Randall (1991), Evans, Orians, and Ascher (1992), and Siminoff and Leonard (1999) all appear to confuse waiting lists with shortages. That confusion, in turn, leads these authors to conclude (incorrectly) that the potential supply of cadaveric donors is insufficient to eliminate the shortage.

28. The death-adjusted shortage is simply the annual increase in the waiting list plus the number of deaths of those patients on the waiting list in that year.

29. The shortage versus backlog distinction is analogous to the distinction between the federal government's annual deficit and the national debt. The former is a flow, while the latter is a stock.

30. This analysis assumes that it would be desirable to replace all living-donor kidney transplants with cadaveric donor organs. In fact, that is probably not the case, because transplant success rates, particularly long term, are significantly higher for the former. At the same time, however, at least some of that observed difference is likely to be attributable to superior tissue matching and reduced eschemic times (the length of time between removal of the transplanted organ and its placement within the organ recipient), both of which would be likely to improve for cadaveric donors if the organ shortage were eliminated.

31. This characteristic of demand applies, *a fortiori,* to other transplantable organs (for example, hearts and livers), as no such substitutable therapy is available.

32. See Gortmaker et al. (1996).

33. Religious or other beliefs may cause some potential donors to place an extremely high value on burying the body intact. These donors are simply located far up the supply curve and are unlikely to sell at any price. Nor are they likely to donate.

34. Of course, the price elasticity of cadaveric organ supply is, ultimately, an empirical question. In chapter 6 we present some tentative empirical evidence that supports the conclusion we have reached here on purely theoretical grounds. That is, the limited survey evidence we have been able to garner on this issue suggests an elastic response to the payment of positive prices.

35. Attempts to increase supply through other, nonprice methods, such as advertising and educational programs, may reduce the shortage by shifting the horizontal intercept of the supply curve to the right. They are unlikely, however, to eliminate the shortage entirely. Indeed, the fact that they have been unable to do so for over thirty years now provides compelling evidence of their inherent inability to correct this problem.

36. See, for example, Evans (1993) and Siminoff and Leonard (1999).

37. A less elastic organ demand would yield a higher black-market price.

38. Technically, P_b provides a lower bound on the prices that black-market suppliers might be able to obtain for illegal kidney sales. Because kidneys are not allocated to the highest bidders under the current system, there are likely to exist some potential recipients willing to pay prices above P_b who have been unable to obtain any of the limited number available legally. As a result, some of these individuals may bid prices well above P_b for black-market kidneys. For a more complete treatment of this point, see Kaserman and Barnett (1991).

39. An offer—as it turns out, a bogus one—to auction off a living-donor kidney on e-Bay recently resulted in (perhaps genuine) bids of over $1 million.

40. Barnett, Saliba, and Walker (2001) make a distinction between an "economic shortage" and a "medical shortage," where they define the former in the traditional manner as the difference between the quantity demanded and the quantity supplied at some below-equilibrium price and the latter as the difference between the quantity demanded and the quantity supplied at a price of zero.

41. It is worth noting that the number of kidney transplants per cadaveric donor has declined substantially over the past ten years. See table 2-4 for more details. The precise cause of this decline is not known at this time.

42. At the same time, improvements in immunosuppressive drugs and surgical techniques have undoubtedly expanded the set of patients for which a transplant is a feasible treatment alternative. As a result, many transplant centers now list patients who would have been turned down on medical grounds in the past. But, as the medical constraints have eased, the shortage constraints have tightened.

43. It is also worth noting that the United Network for Organ Sharing organ allocation criteria apply only to those patients who pass this screening process and are placed on the waiting lists.

44. As noted above, shortages may not have existed in the earliest days of organ transplantation—the late 1950s and the 1960s. In fact, Dr. Thomas Peters informs us that the Southeastern Organ Procurement Foundation was originally created in the late 1960s to facilitate transfers of surplus kidneys between transplant centers. Nonetheless, shortages have persisted since at least the mid- to late 1970s.

45. For a cogent explanation of why additional spending on public education regarding organ donation is unlikely to significantly expand organ supply, see Verble and Worth (1996).

46. For a recent appeal to focus more effort on public education as a strategy to resolve the organ shortage, see Siminoff et al. (2001).

47. On purely theoretical grounds, certain conditions exist under which these two laws may not hold. Because the conditions under which those exceptions can arise are extremely rare, however, we can safely assume that the laws hold for all or virtually all goods, including organs for transplantation.

48. See Pub. L. 98-507, October 19, 1984, 98 Stat. 2339 (Title 42, sec. 273 et seq.).

49. Under the current system, the donor's family is provided very limited information about the recipient (or recipients). The identity of the recipient is withheld to avoid potential problems of emotional or even financial blackmail.

50. See Denise (1985).

51. The effect of this lack of a direct profit incentive for cadaveric organ procurement has apparently been ameliorated somewhat by a de facto policy whereby the Health Care Financing Administration overcompensates hospitals for the cost of organ removal. See Evans (1993). Also, the Health Care Financing Administration imposes certain performance standards on the organ procurement organizations. Failure to meet certain minimum rates of organ collection can result in loss of the organization's franchise.

52. See Chapman (1984, 108) and Denise (1985).

53. Another new drug, first known by its code name, FK-506, and now marketed under the brand name Prograf, may offer even greater promise than cyclosporine. And other new drugs are under development.

54. These are one-year patient survival rates.

55. "The Impact of Cyclosporine on the Practice of Renal Transplantation," *Transplant Proceedings* 21 (1989, 63).

56. See Chapman (1983) and Prottas (1985).

57. As shown in table 2-4, the number of cadaveric donors increased by an average annual rate of only 3.7 percent between 1988 and 1998. The average annual increase from 1990 to 1998 was even smaller—around 3 percent.

58. See Cohen (1989), Siminoff and Leonard (1999), and Sade (1999).

59. See Peters et al. (1996, 2420), who argue that much of the (marginal) growth in cadaveric organ donation in recent years has been due to this expansion of the pool of potential donors.

60. See Prottas (1989, 48).

61. See, for example, Gortmaker et al. (1996).

62. If, as we argued above, demand is somewhat suppressed as a result of relatively stringent screening of transplant candidates, an easing of the shortage may result in a rightward shift in demand. Nonetheless, the potential supply of cadaveric organs still appears sufficient to meet demand, even if that demand were to double.

63. A 1985 Gallup poll found that 73 percent of respondents would be willing to donate the organs of a recently deceased relative. See "Developments in the Law" (1990).

64. See Spieldenner (2000, 1).

65. See U.S. Research Documentation Section, Public Health Service, *RDS 1999 Annual Data Report* at www.med.umich.edu/usrds/chapters/ch03.pdf.

66. See Prottas (1985, 366).

67. See Aroesty and Rettig (1984, 27). More recently, it has been estimated that these savings could reach $25,000 per patient per year. See Rothfeder (1989, 94).

68. There are two basic forms of dialysis—hemodialysis and peritoneal dialysis. The former is used far more often. The problems we identify in the text apply to both hemodialysis and peritoneal dialysis. With hemodialysis, the patient must spend two to five hours a day, three days a week connected to the machine. In addition, when disconnected, patients usually experience a "washed out" feeling for the rest of the day.

69. See Merrill (1978, 343). Perhaps the best indication of the reduced quality of life of the patients undergoing dialysis is the fact that the rate of suicides among

these patients is over 100 times that of the general population. See Cohen (1989, 38).

70. See Mange, Joffee, and Feldman (2001).

71. As noted earlier, some of the long-term differential in success rates may be attributable to the shortage itself (for example, use of poorly matched kidneys). If so, additional convergence of these rates will accompany resolution of the shortage. They appear unlikely to become equal, however, at least within the foreseeable future.

72. The direct (billable) medical costs of living versus cadaveric donor transplants appear to be roughly the same. These costs, however, fail to account for the indirect costs borne by the living donors themselves.

73. In addition to accepting organs from older donors, transplant physicians have also begun to accept organs from non-heart-beating (as opposed to brain-dead) donors and organs with observable medical deficiencies that make them less than ideal for transplantation purposes. See Engstrom (2001). At the same time, medical advances have enabled the successful use of what would have previously been unusable organs.

74. See www.unos.org/Newsroom/critdata_donors.htm.

75. See Williams (1994) and Finkel (2001).

76. Barnett and Kaserman (1998) provide an economic analysis of the artificial incentives for entry created by the shortage.

Chapter 3: Alternative Policy Proposals

1. See Jeffries (1998, 622).

2. The reference section of this monograph provides a fairly comprehensive bibliography of the relevant work.

3. A much less comprehensive list of these articles is contained in the reference section. See, for example, "Forum: Sacred or for Sale?" (1990), Chapman (1984), Clark et al. (1988), Rothfeder (1989), Siebert and Waldrop (1988), Swerdlow and Cate (1990), Finkel (2001), and Engstrom (2001).

4. As with most general statements, there are some exceptions. Some authors continue to defend the current system or some close variant of it. See, for example, Pellegrino (1991), Titmuss (1971), Council of the Transplantation

Society (1985), and Siminoff et al. (2001). Most of the more recent literature, however, advocates some sort of fundamental change.

5. A partial exception to this statement is Childress (1989). Childress, however, does not compare all of the alternative procurement policies discussed here. Moreover, his discussion is limited to ethical considerations alone. As a result, he has little or nothing to say about how these alternative policies would perform in terms of the total number of organs procured.

6. Policy inertia is due to a number of factors, such as uncertainty concerning the effects of proposed changes and the presence of interest groups that hold stakes in—that is, benefit from—the existing policy.

7. If public policy were easily changed, we could experiment with a number of options sequentially and select the one that yields the best performance. Given inertia, however, the costs of selecting a suboptimal policy loom large.

8. See Dukeminier and Sanders (1968).

9. Dworkin (1993, 66) states correctly that "the options available to increase the supply of scarce goods are basically three—donation, conscription, or sale." The six policies described here can be seen as variants of these three fundamental alternatives.

10. For example, procurement of blood uses both market and altruist (donative) methods in tandem. Similarly, organ procurement could easily accommodate an equivalent combination policy in which individuals are free either to donate or to sell. In addition, routine request and required referral would appear to be complementary policy options that could be integrated into a combination with either a market or an altruistic system.

11. Douglass (1996, 213) cites a study that found that between 30 and 47 percent of the families of potential cadaveric organ donors were never asked to consent to donation. Also, of those who were asked, less than 50 percent agreed to donate. Together, these figures are consistent with an effective collection rate of approximately 20 to 30 percent from the pool of potential organ donors. More recent regulations requiring referral of all hospital deaths to organ procurement organizations has undoubtedly improved the first figure (the percentage asked), but apparently it has had no significant impact on the latter figure (the percentage who donate).

12. Our discussion here is rather brief. Those seeking more detailed treatments of the individual policies should consult the relevant literature cited under each alternative.

13. See Douglass (1996, 218).

14. In fact, the Virginia statute, the first of its kind, was passed in response to a physician's attempt to depart from the traditional policy by creating a brokerage firm to buy and sell kidneys from living donors. See Denise (1985). Importantly, however, the National Organ Transplant Act itself makes no distinction between purchases from living donors and purchases of organs obtained from deceased individuals.

15. As noted earlier, it is unclear who, in fact, owns the organs of the deceased. In practice, the property rights in this area are ill-defined. See, generally, Schwindt and Vining (1986, 485–87). These authors point out that problems invariably arise when a valuable asset exists without well-defined property rights. As the organ shortage grows worse, the asset value of transplantable organs increases. The ambiguity of ownership is a major shortcoming of public policy in the organ procurement area. See, also, Douglass (1996) and Jeffries (1998).

16. Under the present system, the donor's family is provided very limited information about the recipient (or recipients). The identity of the recipient is withheld to avoid potential problems of emotional or even financial blackmail. Nonetheless, proposals for so-called directed giving, whereby organ donors are allowed to exercise some control over who the recipients will be, have appeared. See Sade (1999).

17. As we discuss later, the cooperation of hospital personnel in identifying potential donors is now enforced by required referral regulations. In addition, organ procurement organizations have begun to be subjected to certain performance standards to maintain their franchises.

18. See Chapman (1983, 399–400), Cohen (1989, 3–6), and Dukeminier (1970, 813–15).

19. Articles dealing with presumed consent include Butler (1985), Dukeminier (1970), Dukeminier and Sanders (1968), Silver (1988), Spital (1991), Veatch (1991), Gorsline and Johnson (1994), Williams (1994), and Kurnit (1994).

20. As noted in chapter 2, the Uniform Anatomical Gift Act of 1968—adopted by all fifty states by 1972—mandates that a donor's stated preferences are binding after death. See Stuart et al. (1981) and Douglass (1996). After death, the rights of the intended recipient (if one exists) are to dominate the claims of all others under this law. Nonetheless, attending physicians routinely require permission from the patient's family before removing the organs. Such a requirement appears

to violate this act. Such violations have gone unpunished to date, apparently because there is no identifiable plaintiff to enforce compliance.

21. Various forms of presumed consent have been proposed. Under some, the family of the deceased has no authority to permit or deny organ removal. This approach is consistent with the Uniform Anatomical Gift Act.

22. See Kittur et al. (1991, 1443).

23. See Jeffries (1998, 634, n. 7), citing Gorsline and Johnson (1994).

24. See, for example, ibid.

25. Indeed, as Jeffries (1998, 639) points out, for certain organs, Austria's collection rate is equal to or even less than other countries that employ less stringent policies.

26. We are hesitant to say that this policy would increase "donation" rates because organ suppliers do not voluntarily donate organs under this system. *Confiscated* would, perhaps, be a more appropriate term.

27. We are very grateful to Dr. Jay Bhattacharya for urging us to consider this issue in more detail.

28. This amendment states: "No person shall . . . be deprived of life, liberty or property without due process of law; nor shall private property be taken for public use without compensation."

29. It also appears to fail to pass moral or ethical muster. We address that issue in chapter 4.

30. An additional source of economic inefficiency arises if the organ demand curve exhibits a price elasticity greater than zero. In that case, a socially excessive number of organs would be harvested under a conscription policy. We return to this inefficiency later in this chapter.

31. Note the functional similarities between this policy and a policy of conscription. Under both policies, potential donors' families are excluded from the decision process, and some action on the part of the potential donor may be required to prevent organ donation.

32. See Cate (1994, 73).

33. The compensation offered may take any of a variety of forms—an income tax credit, payment toward funeral expenses, or a direct monetary payment. Economic principles suggest that a menu approach in which potential organ donors can select from a set of alternative compensation mechanisms that

includes a direct monetary payment as one of the available options will yield the greatest number of organs, *ceteris paribus.*

34. See Peters (1991).

35. See Kittur et al. (1991, 1442) and Peters et al. (1996).

36. See Peters (1991).

37. See Murray and Youngner (1994, 814).

38. The state of Pennsylvania recently authorized experimentation with a $300 payment toward the funeral expenses of the donor. To our knowledge, however, no such payments have yet been made.

39. Proposals for organ markets are not new. See, for example, Brams (1977), Cohen (1989), Dworkin (1993), Hansmann (1989a), Radcliffe-Richards (1996), Barney and Reynolds (1989), and Blair and Kaserman (1991).

40. Exceptions exist. See, for example, Dworkin (1993) and Amerling (2001).

41. See Blair and Kaserman (1991, 430).

42. See Cohen (1989, 30).

43. This point has been the subject of some confusion in the literature. For example, Siminoff and Leonard (1999, 253) write: "[A]lthough the specifics for proposed market incentive-based systems vary significantly, there are also many points of consensus. The most consistent feature is that of reciprocity: organ donors should be granted some sort of consideration for use of their organs, *and recipients should make some sacrifice in order to receive them.*" (Emphasis added.) Most authors of which we are aware advocate markets for procurement but not distribution.

44. See Aroesty and Rettig (1984, 28–35) and Amerling (2001, 58).

45. In fact, transplant centers already pay a substantial price to organ procurement organizations for the organs they acquire. See Evans (1993).

46. It is likely that the End Stage Renal Disease Program's budget would be reduced by including in the coverage provided the purchase price of kidneys, because of the substantial cost savings realized from transplanting additional dialysis patients. See Aroesty and Rettig (1984, 26–27) and Schwindt and Vining (1986, 491). Moreover, as noted earlier, it is also likely that equilibrium organ prices would be relatively low. See Blair and Kaserman (1991, 446), and Cohen (1989, 35–36).

47. Again, use of the market system to procure organs does not require use of the market system to distribute them among potential recipients.

48. Schwindt and Vining (1986, 489–98) analyze how such a futures market could operate. As they point out, a potential advantage of a futures market is that no negotiations need occur at the time of death. A potential disadvantage of such a market would be the substantial uncertainty of future delivery on the contract, although a system of reporting and information exchange between hospitals and the firms holding the futures contracts may develop to reduce this problem. We return to this issue later in this monograph.

49. In effect, a spot market for cadaveric organs would be financially equivalent to the donor's having a term life insurance policy on which no premiums have been charged.

50. With both a spot market and a futures market, the two prices would be functionally related but clearly not equal. The futures market price would fall well below the spot market price because of both discounting and the extremely low probability of collecting the organs of a given individual. With approximately 2 million deaths in the United States each year and only around 20,000 of those occurring under conditions that would allow organ donation, the probability that an individual's death could potentially yield transplantable organs is only 1 percent. If the equilibrium price of a donor's organs is, say, $1,000, this factor alone would suggest a futures price of only $10, even before discounting for time.

51. See Hansmann (1989b, 57–86). For similar examples, see Cohen (1989, 32–36) and Schwindt and Vining (1986, 489–98).

52. Many organ market proposals use payment schemes that offer organ suppliers "in kind" payments—for example, reductions in insurance premiums or burial expenses, as opposed to cash payments. As noted earlier, a menu approach that offers donors a set of compensation alternatives, including a cash payment, is likely to elicit a greater response.

53. For a more detailed comparison of markets and compensation, see Barnett, Blair, and Kaserman (1992).

54. As noted above, Peters (1991) proposes a payment of $1,000.

55. Barney and Reynolds (1989) apply this sort of welfare analysis to organ markets.

56. For a more detailed explanation of this point, see Kaserman and Barnett (1991).

57. Also, as discussed in chapter 2, it is quite possible that elimination of the shortage may result in an increase in organ demand as the criteria for admission to

the waiting lists are relaxed. This effect, which is not depicted in our figure, would increase substantially the calculated welfare gain associated with organ markets.

58. The expectation of a large supply elasticity is supported both by theoretical considerations (discussed in chapter 2) and by some preliminary empirical evidence (presented in chapter 6).

59. We provide a rough (and very conservative) approximation of the magnitude of the social welfare gain achievable by movement to a market system of organ procurement of kidneys in the appendix to this chapter.

60. Of course, it is possible that more than Q_C organs will be collected under conscription. Such overcollection, however, results in wastage, as no demand exists for these additional organs. Therefore, collection of organs beyond Q_C only makes the conscription alternative worse. Thus, by assuming that only Q_C organs are harvested under this policy, we are tilting the scales of our comparison in favor of conscription.

61. Of course, as demand approaches the perfectly inelastic state, the area C approaches zero.

62. For example, express donation (along with routine request, required referral, and additional expenditures on donor education) could, in principle, shift the horizontal intercept of the organ supply curve to the right until it reaches the horizontal intercept of the organ demand curve. For all practical purposes, however, the probability of that event's occurring is zero. The fact that it has not happened in over thirty years of experience with this policy provides compelling testimony that it will not happen.

63. Interestingly, of all the interest groups affected by organ procurement, transplant candidates (and organ donors) have, perhaps, been the least represented in policy debates. Such underrepresentation, we believe, is readily explained by the economic theory of regulation. See, for example, Stigler (1971), Posner (1971), and Peltzman (1976).

64. Note that giving donors the option of receiving payment in exchange for permission to remove the organs of the deceased does not preclude the personal rewards associated with a purely altruistic (zero-price) donation. Both incentives may combine to motivate supply, just as they currently do in the market for blood procurement. Some comparisons with our experience from blood sales are provided in the appendix to chapter 4.

65. As noted earlier, the National Organ Transplant Act of 1984 was passed primarily in response to lobbying efforts of physicians' groups.

66. Also, while the organ procurement organizations may lose their monopsony status, the need for organ procurement personnel will remain. In fact, as collections increase, the demand for these individuals' services could increase. In addition, the opportunity to earn profits in this business may provide an incentive for those involved in the procurement process to favor the markets alternative, particularly those that are unusually adept at procurement.

67. See Blair and Kaserman (1991).

68. We present a potential (economic) explanation for such a defensive attitude on the part of the medical community in chapter 5.

Chapter 4: Ethical and Economic Objections to Organ Markets

1. See Radcliffe-Richards (1996, 406).

2. See, for example, Council of the Transplantation Society (1985), Pellegrino (1991), Siminoff and Leonard (1999), and Gorsline and Johnson (1994).

3. It is also possible that the success of these arguments is due to the receptiveness or predisposition of the audience to favor arguments opposing organ markets. We return to that issue in chapter 5.

4. See Childress (1989).

5. See ibid., 98.

6. See Jonsen (1988, 219).

7. See Childress (1989, 98).

8. See ibid., 95–98.

9. See Quay (1984, 889).

10. See Caplan (1984, 983).

11. See Mavrodes (1988, 139).

12. See Hansmann (1989a, 72–73).

13. See Schwindt and Vining (1986, 497).

14. See Childress (1989, 110). We should note that the policy advocated by Childress—express donation—has been given thirty years to work, and it has failed. Moreover, while we continue to "give it a chance," thousands of people are dying.

15. The empirical evidence that exists regarding these two issues, while limited, tends to reject both claims. See the appendix to this chapter and the evidence presented in chapter 6.

16. See Radin (1996).

17. See ibid., 51.

18. See ibid., 97.

19. See Titmuss (1970) and Thorne (1998).

20. See Radzik and Schmidtz (1999, 607).

21. See ibid.

22. See ibid.

23. See Arrow (1997, 764).

24. The list of so-called ethical issues with which we deal here is far from exhaustive. Other arguments of an ethical nature can be found in the extant literature. See, for example, Blair and Kaserman (1991). The three issues discussed here, however, appear to be the most common ones. Our intention is not to rebut all possible ethical objections to organ markets but to suggest the basic lack of logical support that exists for such objections.

25. These arguments have been considered and rejected by others. See, for example, Radcliffe-Richards (1996) and Dworkin (1993).

26. *Webster's New Collegiate Dictionary,* 6th ed., provides the following definitions of the word *coerce:* "1: to restrain or dominate by nullifying individual will 2: to compel to an act or choice <they could ~ the citizens by threats but not persuade their agreement> 3: to enforce or bring about by force or threat." A voluntary transaction between two willing parties clearly does not qualify as coercion under any of these definitions.

27. This point is emphasized by Radcliffe-Richards (1996, 377): "Our indignation on behalf of the exploited poor seems to take the curious form of wanting to make them worse off still." And later, she writes: "[P]revention of sales, in itself, only closes a miserable range of options still further. To the coercion of poverty is added the coercion of the supposed protector" (382).

28. Moreover, the current system fosters an undesirable atmosphere of emotional coercion within families. Living related donors may agree to donate only under intense pressure from family members. As a result, decreased reliance on living related donors under a market system would reduce coercion from this source.

29. Note that this argument also assumes a relatively high market-clearing price of organs.

30. Under a futures market approach, the deceased will have already received whatever compensation has been paid to encourage the donation. In that event, the surviving family members hold no property rights, because these have already been purchased by an organ procurement firm. Thus, under this scenario, concerns regarding premature termination of care should vanish.

31. Barnett and Kaserman (1995) provide an economic analysis of the relationship between the shortage and the incentive to enter the transplant business.

32. Those who prefer the altruistic system rarely offer any persuasive economic objections to a market system. More typical is some conclusory statement without much support. See, for example, "Regulating the Gift of Life" (1990), asserting that "[t]he present altruistic system offers social benefits that outweigh the speculative increase in organ supply promised by adding financial incentives."

33. Those making this claim generally state it as a theoretical possibility rather than an empirical reality. The existence and significance of this potential effect, however, ultimately constitute an empirical question.

34. See Managa (1987), explaining the logic of this reaction: "The commercialization of organs . . . affects the meaning of the gift to the donor. When unpriced, it is often perceived to be a 'priceless' gift essential to the saving of a life. With its commercialization it has a price, one which merely denotes how much a donor is saving the procurement agency should he decide to donate it rather than sell it." As a result, "the pricing of organs may be said to diminish the value and meaning of the voluntary donation of organs."

35. See our discussion of the evidence pertaining to blood sales in the appendix to this chapter and our survey results relating to organ markets reported in chapter 6. Both these sources of evidence support the conclusion that any such discontinuity is small.

36. Rose-Ackerman (1985) points to quality control as a possible justification for modified inalienability, which permits donations but does not permit sales.

37. Rose-Ackerman (1985, 947) also recognizes that "undersupply may continue to be a serious problem."

38. Douglass (1996, 202) writes:

While in a majority of cases the donated organ truly is the "gift of life," many recipients have been transplanted with deadly organs resulting from pitfalls in the organ donation process. By 1993, 6,798 patients were documented as recipients of cancerous organs, and it is estimated that the cancer incidence in patients who undergo transplantation ranges from 4% to 18%.

According to Douglass, this problem is attributable to both the desperation caused by the shortage and the "good faith" indemnification from liability for organ procurers provided by the law. See, also, Engstrom (2001).

39. See Radcliffe-Richards (1996, 390).

40. Dworkin's (1993, 69) conclusion regarding markets for living donors should hold a *fortiori* for cadaveric donor markets.

41. See, especially, Titmuss (1972).

42. Titmuss's (1972) book sparked a widespread debate among economists, legal scholars, and medical professionals. See, for example, Kessel (1974), Arrow (1975), and Havighurst (1977).

43. See Upton (1973).

44. See Hansmann (1989a, 68 n. 23).

45. As Hansmann (1989a, 68 n. 23) noted, a low payment may send a signal to donors that the blood they have been giving actually has a correspondingly low social value and may thereby discourage them from continuing to supply blood.

46. Arrow (1975, 28) concludes: "I see . . . no real evidence that the presence of a commercial blood supply decreases the amount of altruism."

47. See Titmuss (1972) and Oswalt (1977, 123), who cites Allen (1972).

48. See Kessel (1974).

49. Such indemnification was provided by a series of state laws passed in the early 1970s. Those laws were enacted in response to a lawsuit brought in Illinois by a patient who had contracted hepatitis after receiving a transfusion. See Kessel (1974, 277). See, also, Havighurst (1977).

50. Two of these have been noted in the prior literature. See Cohen (1989, 29 n. 91) and Hansmann (1989a, 68 n. 23).

51. See Cohen (1989, 20, n. 91).

52. See ibid.

53. Assurance programs promise blood donors that they and their family or group will receive any blood they may require free of charge for some specified period of time. In effect, these programs are equivalent to an insurance policy for future blood needs. See Oswalt (1977, 126). Tabarrok (2002) has proposed such an assurance program for organ procurement.

Chapter 5: The Medical Community's Opposition to Organ Markets

1. See Evans (1993, 3117).

2. As noted in chapter 3, that opposition appears to be waning somewhat as the tragedies caused by the shortage continue to mount. Nonetheless, the predominant view of the medical and transplant community remains opposed to organ markets.

3. See Schwindt and Vining (1986). Transplant specialists represent a small constituency within the American Medical Association. Nevertheless, the association has an incentive to promote the interest of even a very small constituency if such activities are not detrimental to the interest of other members. And, in this case, the general interest of AMA members may be served by the appearance that physicians support altruism over financial inducements.

4. See Denise (1985).

5. Radcliffe-Richards (1996, 375) writes: "The prohibition of organ sales is derived not from the principles and arguments usually invoked in support of prohibition, but rather, from strong feelings of repugnance which exert an invisible but powerful influence on the debate, distorting the arguments [and working] to the detriment of the [very] people most in need of protection." (Bracketed words in the original.)

6. See Peters et al. (1996), Adams, Barnett, and Kaserman (1999), and Radcliffe-Richards et al. (1998).

7. See Radcliffe-Richards (1996). Because of its strong political influence, that community has also played the predominant role in determining public policy in this area and, thereby, in preserving the current system.

8. In theory, such rents also may be captured by purchasers of the affected output—in this case, taxpayers—if the below-market price of the input is passed through by suppliers of downstream services. Such an outcome, however, seems

unlikely in this case, given the relative abilities of the various groups involved to capture these rents.

9. The model we present here is a simplification of the more complex analysis contained in Barnett, Beard, and Kaserman (1993). The basic findings, however, are the same.

10. Transplants and organs generally exhibit a fixed input-output ratio equal to one. That is, a one-to-one relationship exists between the organ input and transplant output.

11. For reasons discussed earlier, the slope of this curve above the zero price is expected to be relatively low; that is, the supply curve is expected to be relatively price elastic.

12. At the same time, our conclusions are not dependent on a strict correspondence between market conditions and these features.

13. Strict equality between the increased quantities in the two markets as well as the increase in the marginal costs of transplants and the price of organs is attributable to the fixed input-output ratio of one assumed here. Again, however, our basic conclusions are not dependent on this assumption.

14. These fees, which vary somewhat by region to reflect labor cost differences, are essentially set on a cost-plus or average cost basis. A typical payment by HCFA for a kidney transplant in the late 1980s was around $40,000 and was not predicated on transplant success, hospitalization duration, transplant volume, or other similar factors.

15. Obviously, the magnitude of these profits depends on the difference between $\bar{P}_T$ and MC_T, as well as the number of transplants performed. As noted earlier, indirect evidence in the form of rapid entry into the transplant business during the 1980s and 1990s suggests that such profits have been substantial. See Barnett and Kaserman (1995).

Notice, in this figure, that shifting Q_0 to the right—increasing donations at the zero price—is always profitable if the marginal cost of increasing altruistic donations is less than $\bar{P}_T$ or if another party (for example, the government) bears those costs. On this basis, then, the medical community's support for additional spending on educational initiatives to increase altruistic donations is easily understood.

16. The incentive to extract rents in performing transplant procedures may exist whether hospitals operate on a for-profit or not-for-profit basis. In the latter case,

rents extracted in one activity can be used to subsidize other desired activities. Such rents also increase opportunities for hospital administrators to engage in utility-maximizing discretionary behavior. Indeed, such agency problems may well be greater in not-for-profit hospitals. In addition, transplant surgeons may capture some of these rents.

17. See, for example, Evans (1993).

18. See, for example, Caplan (1984).

19. The relevant welfare diagrams are straightforward; therefore, we do not present them here.

20. We are grateful to the members of the American Enterprise Institute workshop who reviewed a previous draft of this manuscript for pointing some of these out.

21. For more recent philosophical views on these issues, see Radcliffe-Richards (1996) and Dworkin (1993).

22. We are not arguing here that adoption of the organ market alternative should be put on hold indefinitely until all uncertainty on the part of all parties is resolved. It is imperative that we keep in mind that, while these trials are pro-ceeding, more people are dying. As a result, the social costs of such trials are exceedingly high.

23. All of the above considerations—both economic and noneconomic—help to explain the ubiquity of the observed, virtually worldwide, opposition to organ markets among this group.

Chapter 6: The Question of Supply

This chapter draws heavily from Adams, Barnett, and Kaserman (1999).

1. See Murray and Youngner (1994, 814).

2. Demand is also unlikely to be affected by incomes or the prices of related goods because of third-party payments and the absence of close substitutes.

3. As noted earlier, these demand curves may shift outward if the organ short-age is resolved, because part of the current rationing process involves relatively stringent screening of patients who are admitted to the waiting lists.

4. Importantly, several of these ethical arguments assume implicitly that market-clearing prices for cadaveric organs would be high (in the tens of thou-

sands of dollars). Consequently, the ethical and economic issues surrounding this topic are not entirely independent.

5. We have, nonetheless, drawn the demand curve with a negative slope here to allow for the (highly unlikely) possibility that creation of an organ market might result in fewer organs being collected. This (probably invalid) assumption is necessary to give credence to arguments advanced by opponents of organ markets.

6. If demand is perfectly inelastic (that is, vertical) over the price range from $P = 0$ to $P = P^e_2$, then $Q^e_2 = Q^e_1 = Q^D_0$. The only difference between the various equilibria in that case would be in the market-clearing price that emerges.

7. See Peters (1991).

8. For a technical treatment of the concept of willingness to pay versus willingness to accept, see Haneman (1991).

9. For example, see Caplan (1984), Task Force on Organ Transplantation (1986), and Pellegrino (1991).

10. Note that our definition of this term excludes those who may be somewhat offended but, nonetheless, choose to supply anyway.

11. This basic finding appears to be consistent with our review of the evidence from the market for blood. See the appendix to chapter 4. In addition, it would appear likely that the percentage of individuals who are offended by payments to donors would decline over time as people become accustomed to such payments.

12. Recall that, as discussed in chapter 2, a shortage is measured as a flow rather than a stock. That is, as the difference between the quantity demanded and the quantity supplied at a given price—both of which are flows—a shortage must be expressed as some quantity *per some unit of time*. Thus, the annual shortage of a given organ is not, in general, equal to the backlog of patients appearing on waiting lists. This latter figure is a stock that has accumulated from annual shortages over a number of years.

13. As noted earlier, it is likely that some reliance on living-donor kidneys will remain even in the absence of a shortage. Success rates—particularly long-term— are generally higher with living-donor transplants. The observed difference, however, may itself be at least partially attributable to the existing shortage. For example, poorer matching with cadaveric donors (which could be largely eliminated with an increased supply) may account for at least some of this difference. Nonetheless, we assume here that all living-donor transplants are replaced with

cadaveric donors. Obviously, this assumption will bias our estimate of the market-clearing price upward.

14. Importantly, such an increase in the number of cadaveric donors appears to be well within the range of estimates of potential donor supply. See our discussion of these estimates in chapter 2.

15. Note that 35 percent (138/391) of our sample are willing to donate at a zero price. This figure is well within the range of prior estimates of current donation rates. Also, because this question focuses on the smallest amount the respondent would be willing to accept to donate his or her organs, an upward-biased estimate of the true supply price is expected. Again, this bias is conservative in that it will tend to inflate our estimate of the market-clearing price.

16. Some excess supply will be desirable for some period of time to eliminate the backlog of excess demand that has accumulated from the prior years of shortage. Also, as noted earlier, elimination of the shortage may also cause an increase in demand as criteria for admission to waiting lists are relaxed. Therefore, a portion of this excess supply could also go to satisfy that higher demand.

17. Interestingly, Peters (1991) proposed a financial incentive of $1,000 per donor. Our results, then, suggest that such a level of compensation would completely resolve the organ shortage. Had that proposal been adopted five years ago, more than 15,000 lives could have been saved in the interim. At the same time, it is important to recognize that compensation and organ markets are not equivalent policy options. They are likely to produce distinctly different results. See Barnett, Blair, and Kaserman (1992).

18. This assumption also results in an upward-biased estimate of market-clearing prices.

Chapter 7: Some Thoughts on How Organ Markets Might Operate

1. See Reynolds and Barney (1988, 578).

2. That is not to say that markets always work perfectly or that they should never be constrained in any way. Antitrust laws, property rights, and so on place boundaries on acceptable market conduct.

3. For example, there has been some discussion of whether cadaveric organ markets should be designed to operate on a spot or a futures basis. Commodities

markets typically operate on both. No obvious reason exists for public policy to rule out or even favor either of those options. Market forces should be permitted to adopt whatever form is most efficient. We return to the spot-versus-futures-market issue below.

4. At the same time, there appear to be no compelling grounds—either ethical or economic—on which to base a legal ban on living-organ sales. See, for example, Dworkin (1993). There may, however, be economic forces that would limit the size of such a market. We return to this issue later.

5. See, for example, Schwindt and Vining (1986), Cohen (1989), and Hansmann (1989a).

6. See Peters (1991).

7. We recognize that, because compensation does not involve any restructuring of the current system beyond a relaxation of the constraint that financial inducements cannot be provided, it may appear to be easier and, therefore, faster to implement this policy option. That, however, may very well not be the case. Once they are allowed to be set in motion, market forces can achieve extremely rapid results. Recall, for example, that it was the spontaneous emergence of such forces in response to the organ shortage that led to enactment of the National Organ Transplant Act in 1984.

8. The observed difference in long-term success rates plausibly could diminish if the organ shortage were eliminated by cadaveric organ sales. With an adequate number of cadaveric organs available, improved tissue matching and reduced eschemic times—both of which contribute to transplant success rates—could potentially be achieved. Nonetheless, some difference would likely remain.

9. The data are based on United Network for Organ Sharing–Organ Procurement and Transplantation Network Scientific Registry data as of September 18, 2000.

10. To some extent, this difference in long-term success rates may be at least partially overcome with subsequent cadaveric donor transplants. It is medically feasible to receive more than one renal transplant over a patient's lifetime. Thus, if one graft fails, subsequent transplants sometimes may be performed. Success rates, however, tend to decline with the number of kidney transplants a patient has received.

11. Presumably, most living *related* donors would continue to provide organs to their relatives without (direct) compensation. The bulk of living-donor market transactions would, therefore, likely involve unrelated donors.

12. One of the authors of this monograph has a friend who donated a kidney to his brother some years ago. The brother died within a fairly short period of time, and now the donor has learned that he, too, will need a kidney transplant within the next few years. Not surprisingly, his relatives are reluctant to come forward to donate a kidney to him.

13. A number of payment options have been proposed, including cash, discounts on insurance premiums, payment to estates at death, and so on.

14. Transaction costs are simply the costs of conducting a market exchange. Typically, these costs consist of search costs, negotiation costs, and enforcement costs. See Coase (1937), Williamson (1971), and Blair and Kaserman (1983, chap. 2). Theoretically, transaction costs "drive a wedge" between supply and demand curves and cause the full price paid by the buyer to exceed the price received by the seller.

15. Of course, markets are able to devise efficient methods not only to minimize production costs but to economize on transaction costs as well. Indeed, transaction costs are not an important impediment to the successful functioning of other mortality contingent contracts, such as annuities markets and reverse mortgage markets. Thus, while we expect large transaction costs to be associated with futures market exchange of cadaveric organs, that expectation may not be realized.

16. See Altman (1994).

Chapter 8: Summary and a Call for Action

1. See Williams (1994, 336).

References

Adams, A. Frank, III, A. H. Barnett, and David L. Kaserman. 1999. "Markets for Organs: The Question of Supply." *Contemporary Economic Policy* 17 (April): 147-55.

Allen, J. G. 1972. "Vitae Custodes—The Volunteer Blood Donors." *Nursing Outlook* 20: 588.

Altman, Jason. 1994. "Organ Transplantations: The Need for an International Open Organ Market." *Touro International Law Review* 5: 161–83.

Amerling, Richard. 2001. "Remove Price Controls to Relieve the Shortage." *Transplant News and Issues* 2 (May): 57–58.

Aroesty, Jerome, and Richard A. Rettig. 1984. "The Cost Effects of Improved Kidney Transplantation." RAND Report R-30099-NH/RC.

Arrow, Kenneth J. 1975. "Gifts and Exchanges." In E. Phelps, ed., *Altruism, Morality, and Economic Theory*. New York: Russell Sage Foundation.

———. 1997. "Invaluable Goods." *Journal of Economic Literature* 35 (June): 757–65.

Barnett, A. H., and David L. Kaserman. 1993. "The Shortage of Organs for Transplantation: Exploring the Alternatives." *Issues in Law and Medicine* 9 (Fall): 117–37.

———. 1995. "The 'Rush to Transplant' and Organ Shortages." *Economic Inquiry* 33 (July): 506–15. Reprinted in Bernard Saffran and F. M. Scherer, eds., *Price Theory and Its Applications*. Cheltenham, U.K.: Edward Elgar Publishing, 1998.

———. 2000. "Comment on 'The Shortage in Market-Inalienable Human Organs: A Consideration of 'Nonmarket' Failures—Faulty Analysis of a Failed Policy." *American Journal of Economics and Sociology* 59 (April): 335–49.

Barnett, A. H., T. Randolph Beard, and David L. Kaserman. 1993. "The Medical Community's Opposition to Organ Markets: Ethics or Economics?" *Review of Industrial Organization* 8 (December): 669–78.

———. 1996. "An Extension of 'Scope, Learning, and Cross-Subsidy: Organ Transplants in a Multi-Division Hospital.'" *Southern Economic Journal* 62 (January): 760–67.

Barnett, A. H., Roger D. Blair, and David L. Kaserman. 1992. "Improving Organ Donation: Compensation versus Markets." *Inquiry* 29: 669–78.

———. 1996. "The Economics and Ethics of Organ Markets." *Society* 33 (September/October): 8–17. Reprinted in Alexander Tabarrok, ed., *Entrepreneurial Economics: Bright Ideas from the Dismal Science.* New York: Oxford University Press, 2002.

Barnett, William, II, Michael Saliba, and Deborah Walker. 2001. "A Free Market in Kidneys: Efficient and Equitable." *Independent Review* 5 (Winter): 373–85.

Barney, L. Dwayne, and R. Larry Reynolds. 1989. "An Economic Analysis of Transplant Organs." *Atlantic Economic Journal* 17: 12–20.

Blair, Roger D., and David L. Kaserman. 1983. *Law and Economics of Vertical Integration and Control.* New York: Academic Press.

———. 1991. "The Economics and Ethics of Alternative Cadaveric Organ Procurement Policies." *Yale Journal on Regulation* 8 (Summer): 403–52.

Brams, Marvin. 1977. "Transplantable Organs: Should Their Sale Be Authorized by State Statutes?" *American Journal of Law and Medicine* 3 (2): 183–95.

Browning, Edgar K., and Mark A. Zupan. 1999. *Microeconomics: Theory and Applications.* New York: Wiley.

Butler, Michael J. 1985. "The Law of Human Organ Procurement: A Modest Proposal." *Journal of Contemporary Health Law and Policy* 1: 195–206.

Caplan, Arthur. 1984. "Ethical and Policy Issues in the Procurement of Cadaveric Organs for Transplantation." *New England Journal of Medicine* 311: 981–83.

Cate, Fred H. 1994. "Human Organ Transplantation: The Role of Law." *Journal of Corporation Law* 20 (Fall): 69–90.

Chapman, David E. 1983. "Retaining Human Organs under the Uniform Commercial Code." *Marshall Law Review* 16: 393–417.

Chapman, Fern Schumer. 1984. "The Life-and-Death Question of an Organ Market." *Fortune* (June 11): 108–18.

Childress, James F. 1989. "Ethical Criteria for Procuring and Distributing Organs for Transplantation." *Journal of Health, Politics, Policy, and Law* 14 (Spring): 87–113.

Clark, Matt, et al. 1988. "Interchangeable Parts." *Newsweek* (September 12): 61, 63.

Coase, Ronald. 1937. "The Nature of the Firm." *Economica* 4 (November): 386–405.

Cohen, Lloyd R. 1989. "Increasing the Supply of Transplant Organs: The Virtues of a Futures Market." *George Washington Law Review* 58 (November): 1–51.

Council of the Transplantation Society. 1985. "Commercialization in Transplantation: The Problems and Some Guidelines for Practice." *Lancet* 2: 715–16.

Denise, Susan H. 1985. "Regulating the Sale of Human Organs." *Virginia Law Review* (Spring): 1015–38.

"Developments in the Law: Medical Technology and the Law." 1990. *Harvard Law Review* 102: 1519–1676.

Douglass, Lisa E. 1996. "Organ Donation, Procurement, and Transplantation: The Process, the Problems, the Law." *University of Missouri—Kansas City Law Review* 65: 201–30.

Dukeminier, Jesse, Jr. 1970. "Supplying Organs for Transplantation." *Michigan Law Review* 68: 811–65.

Dukeminier, Jesse, Jr., and David Sanders. 1968. "Organ Transplantation: A Proposal for Routine Salvaging of Cadaver Organs." *New England Journal of Medicine* 279 (August 22): 413–19.

Dworkin, Gerald. 1993. "Markets and Morals: The Case for Organ Sales." *Mount Sinai Journal of Medicine* 60 (January): 66–69.

Eilperin, Juliet. 2000. "House Acts to Reject Rules on Transplants; Voting 275-147, Lawmakers Side with Private Network in Dispute with HHS." *Washington Post*, April 5.

Ekelund, Robert B., and Robert D. Tollison. 1994. *Economics: Private Markets and Public Choice.* Reading, Mass.: Addison-Wesley.

Engstrom, Paul. 2001. "Damaged Goods." *Washington Post,* June 26.

Evans, Roger W. 1993. "Organ Procurement Expenditures and the Role of Financial Incentives." *Journal of the American Medical Association* 269: 3113–18.

Evans, Roger W., Carlyn E. Orians, and Nancy L. Ascher. 1992. "The Potential Supply of Organ Donors: An Assessment of the Efficiency of Organ Procurement Efforts in the United States." *Journal of the American Medical Association* 267 (January 8): 239–46.

Finkel, Michael. 2001. "This Little Kidney Went to Market." *New York Times Magazine,* May 27.

"Forum: Sacred or for Sale?" 1990. *Harper's Monthly*, October, 47–55.

Gorsline, Monique C., and Rachelle K. Johnson. 1994. "The United States System of Organ Donation, the International Solution, and the Cadaveric Organ Donor Act: 'And the Winner Is . . .'." *Journal of Corporation Law*, 20 (Fall): 5–46.

Gortmaker, Steven L., et al. 1996. "Organ Donor Potential and Performance: Size and Nature of the Organ Donor Shortfall." *Critical Care Medicine* 24: 432–39.

"Great Success with Drug in Transplant of Organs." 1989. *New York Times*, October 18.

Haneman, W. Michael. 1991. "Willingness to Pay and Willingness to Accept: How Much Can They Differ?" *American Economic Review* 81 (June): 635–47.

Hansmann, Henry. 1989a. "The Economics and Ethics of Markets for Human Organs." *Journal of Health, Politics, Policy, and Law* (Spring): 57–85.

———. 1989b. "The Economics and Ethics of Markets for Human Organs." In James F. Blumstein and Frank A. Sloan, eds., *Organ Transplantation Policy: Issues and Prospects*. Durham, N.C.: Duke University Press, 57–86.

Havighurst, Clark C., 1977. "Legal Responses to the Problem of Poor-Quality Blood." In David B. Johnson, ed., *Blood Policy: Issues and Alternatives*. Washington, D.C.: American Enterprise Institute.

Hull, Alan. 1990. "U.S. Donor Procurement in 1989: Same Song, Third Verse." *Nephrology News and Issues* (March): 32–35.

Jeffries, David E. 1998. "The Body as Commodity: The Use of Markets to Cure the Organ Deficit." *Global Legal Studies Journal* 5: 621–58.

Jonsen, Albert R. 1988. "Transplantation of Fetal Tissue: An Ethicist's Viewpoint." *Clinical Research* 36: 215–19.

Kaserman, David L., and A. H. Barnett. 1991. "An Economic Analysis of Transplant Organs: A Comment and Extension." *Atlantic Economic Journal* 19 (June): 57–63.

Kessel, Reuben, 1974. "Transfused Blood, Serum Hepatitis, and the Coase Theorem." *Journal of Law and Economics* 17 (October): 265–89.

Kittur, Dilip S., et al. 1991. "Incentives for Organ Donation." *Lancet* 338: 1441–43.

Kurnit, Melissa N. 1994. "Organ Donation in the United States: Can We Learn from Successes Abroad?" *Boston College International and Comparative Law Review* 17 (Summer): 405–52.

Lee, Paul P. 1986. "The Organ Supply Dilemma: Acute Shortage." *Columbia Journal of Law and Social Problems* 20 (4): 363–407.

Managa, A. 1987. "A Commercial Market for Organs? Why Not?" *Bioethics* 1: 321.

Mange, Kevin C., Marshall M. Joffee, and Harold I. Feldman. 2001. "Effect of the Use or Nonuse of Long-Term Dialysis on the Subsequent Survival of Renal Transplants from Living Donors." *New England Journal of Medicine* 344 (March 8): 726–31.

Mavrodes, George I. 1980. "The Morality of Selling Human Organs." *Ethics, Humanism, and Medicine:* 133–39.

———. 1988. "The Morality of Selling Human Organs." *Journal of Health Care Marketing* 8: 72.

———. 1989. "The Morality of Selling Human Organs: What Price Consent?" *Clinical and Biological Research* 38: 133.

Merrill, John P. 1978. "Dialysis versus Transplantation in the Treatment of End-Stage Renal Disease." *Annual Review of Medicine* 29: 343–58.

Murray, Thomas H., and Stuart J. Youngner. 1994. "Organ Salvage Policies: A Need for Better Data and More Insightful Ethics." *Journal of the American Medical Association* 272 (September 14): 814–16.

Oswalt, R. M. 1977. "A Review of Blood Donor Motivation and Recruitment." *Transfusion* 17: 123–35.

Pellegrino, Edmund D. 1991. "Families' Self-Interest and the Cadaver's Organs." *Journal of the American Medical Association* 265 (March 13): 1305–6.

Peltzman, Sam. 1976. "Toward a More General Theory of Regulation." *Journal of Law and Economics* 19 (2): 211–40.

Pessemier, Edgar A., Albert C. Bemmaor, and Dominique M. Hansens. 1977. "Willingness to Supply Human Body Parts: Some Empirical Results." *Journal of Consumer Research* 4 (December): 131–40.

Peters, Thomas G. 1991. "Life or Death: The Issue of Payment in Cadaveric Organ Donations." *Journal of the American Medical Association* 265 (March 13): 1302–5.

Peters, Thomas G., Dilip S. Kittur, L. J. McGaw, M. Roy First, and Edward W. Nelson. 1996. "Organ Donors and Nondonors: An American Dilemma." *Archives of Internal Medicine* 156 (November 25): 2419–24.

Posner, Richard A. 1971. "Taxation by Regulation." *Bell Journal of Economics and Management Science* 2 (1): 22–50.

Prottas, Jeffery M. 1985. "The Structure and Effectiveness of the U.S. Organ Procurement System." *Inquiry* 22: 365–76.

————. 1989. "The Organization of Organ Procurement." In James F. Blumstein and Frank A. Sloan, eds., *Organ Transplantation Policy: Issues and Prospects.* Durham, N.C.: Duke University Press, 41–55.

Quay, Paul M. 1984. "Utilizing the Bodies of the Dead." *St. Louis University Law Journal* 28: 889.

Radcliffe-Richards, Janet. 1996. "Nefarious Goings On: Kidney Sales and Moral Arguments." *Journal of Medicine and Philosophy* 21: 375–416.

Radcliffe-Richards, Janet, A. S. Daer, R. D. Guttman, R. Hoffenberg, I. Kennedy, M. Lock, R. A. Sells, and N. Tilney. 1998. "The Case for Allowing Kidney Sales." *Lancet* 351 (June 27): 1950–52.

Radin, Margaret Jane. 1996. *Contested Commodities.* Cambridge: Harvard University Press, 1996.

Radzik, Linda, and David Schmidtz. 1999. "Contested Commodities." *Law and Philosophy* 16: 603–16.

Randall, Teri. 1991. "Too Few Human Organs for Transplantation, Too Many in Need . . . and the Gap Widens." *Journal of the American Medical Association* 265: 1223–25.

Reels, L., et al. 1990. "Effect of a 'Presumed Consent' Law on Organ Retrieval in Belgium." *Transplant Procedure* 22: 2078?

"Regulating the 'Gift of Life': The 1987 Uniform Anatomical Gift Act: Note." 1990. *Washington Law Review* 65: 171–81.

Rettig, Richard A. 1989. "The Politics of Organ Transplantation: A Parable of Our Time." *Journal of Health, Politics, Policy, and Law* 14 (Spring): 191–227.

Reynolds, R. Larry, and L. Dwayne Barney. 1988. "Economics of Organ Procurement and Allocation." *Journal of Economic Issues* 22 (June): 571–79.

Rose-Ackerman, Susan. 1985. "Inalienability and the Theory of Property Rights." *Columbia Law Review* 65: 931–90.

Rothfeder, Jeffrey. 1989. "Heart Transplants: The Beat Picks Up." *Business Week,* August 28, 94–95.

Sade, Robert M. 1999. "Cadaveric Organ Donation: Rethinking Donor Motivation." *Archives of Internal Medicine* 159 (March 8): 438–42.

Schwindt, Richard, and Aidan R. Vining. 1986. "Proposal for a Future Delivery Market for Transplant Organs." *Journal of Health, Politics, Policy, and Law* 11 (Fall): 483–500.

Siebert, Sam, and Theresa Waldrop. 1988. "Kidney for Sale: The Issue Is Tissue." *Newsweek,* December 5, 38.

Silver, Theodore. 1988. "The Case for a Post-Mortem Organ Draft and a Proposed Organ Draft Act." *Boston University Law Review* 68: 681–728.

Siminoff, Laura A., and Matthew D. Leonard. 1999. "Financial Incentives: Alternatives to the Altruistic Model of Organ Donation." *Journal of Transplant Coordination* 9 (December): 250–56.

Siminoff, Laura A., Nahida Gordon, Joan Hewlett, and Robert M. Arnold. 2001. "Factors Influencing Families' Consent for Donation of Solid Organs for Transplantation." *Journal of the American Medical Association* 286: 71–77.

Spieldenner, Bob. 2000. "Deaths Increase Despite Rise in Number of Transplants." *UNOS Update* (May): 1.

Spital, Aaron. 1991. "The Shortage of Organs for Transplantation: Where Do We Go from Here?" *New England Journal of Medicine* 325 (October 24): 1243–46.

Steinbrook, Robert L. 1981. "Kidneys for Transplantation." *Journal of Health, Politics, Policy, and Law* 6: 504–19.

Stigler, George J. 1971. "The Theory of Economic Regulation." *Bell Journal of Economics and Management Science* 2 (1): 3–21.

Stuart, Frank P., et al. 1981. "Brain Death Laws and Patterns of Consent to Remove Organs for Transplantation from Cadavers in the United States and 28 Other Countries." *Transplantation* 31: 231, 238–44.

Swerdlow, Joel L., and Fred H. Cate. 1990. "Why Transplants Don't Happen." *Atlantic Monthly,* October, 99.

Tabarrok, Alexander. 2002. "The Organ Shortage: A Tragedy of the Commons." In Alexander Tabarrok, ed., *Entrepreneurial Economics: Bright Ideas from the Dismal Science.* New York: Oxford University Press, 107–11.

Task Force on Organ Transplantation. 1986. "Organ Transplantation: Issues and Recommendations."

Thorne, Emanuel D. 1990. "Tissue Transplants: The Dilemma of the Body's Growing Value." *Public Interest* 98 (Winter): 37–48.

Titmuss, Richard M. 1972. *The Gift Relationship: From Human Blood to Social Policy.* New York: Vintage Books.

Upton, W., III. 1973. "Altruism, Attribution, and Intrinsic Motivation in the Recruitment of Blood Donors." In *Selected Readings in Donor Motivation and Recruitment,* vol. 2. Washington, D.C.: American Red Cross.

Veatch, Robert M. 1991. "Routine Inquiry about Organ Donation—An Alternative to Presumed Consent." *New England Journal of Medicine* 325: 1246–49.

Verble, Margaret, and Judy Worth. 1996. "The Case against More Public Education to Promote Organ Donation." *Journal of Transplant Coordination* 6 (December): 200–203.

Williams, Christian. 1994. "Combating the Problems of Human Rights Abuses and Inadequate Organ Supply through Presumed Donative Consent." *Case Western Reserve Journal of International Law* 26 (Spring–Summer): 315–64.

Williamson, Oliver E. 1971. "The Vertical Integration of Production: Market Failure Consideration." *American Economic Review* 61 (May): 112–23.

Wolfe, Robert A., Valarie B. Ashby, Edgar L. Milford, Akinlolu O. Ojo, Robert E. Ettenger, Lawrence Y. C. Agodoa, Philip J. Held, and Friedrich K. Port. 1999. "Comparison of Mortality in All Patients on Dialysis, Patients on Dialysis Awaiting Transplantation, and Recipients of a First Cadaveric Transplant." *New England Journal of Medicine* 341 (December 2): 1725–30.

Index

Adams, A. Frank, III, 156n6, 158
Allen, J. G., 155n47
Allocation concerns, 3, 13, 51, 78
Altman, Jason, 131, 138n24
Altruistic procurement policy, 7, 96
  as cause of shortage, 29–30
  economic comparison with
    market, 92–96
  failure of, 32
  history of, 27–28
  reasons for its longevity, 134–36
American Hospital Association, 61, 90
American Medical Association, 51, 61,
  90, 156n3
Amerling, Richard, 138n17, 149nn40,
  44
Aroesty, Jerome, 144n67, 149nn44,
  46
Arrow, Kenneth J., 75, 155nn42, 46
Ascher, Nancy L., 137n12, 141n27
Auburn University, 106, 107
Austria, 46, 47

Barnett, A. H., 142nn38, 40, 145n76,
  150nn53, 56, 154n31, 156n6,
  157nn9, 15, 160n17
Barney, L. Dwayne, 122, 149n39,
  150n55, 160n1
Beard, Randolph, 157n9
Belgium, 46
Bhattacharya, Jay, 148n27
Black market, 21–22, 38, 95, 138n24

Blair, Roger D., 139, 149nn39, 41,
  46, 150n53, 152n67,
  153n24, 160n17, 162n14
Blood sales, 85–87, 146n10, 151n64,
  154n35
  relevance to organ markets,
    87–88
Brams, Marvin, 149n39
Browning, Edgar K., 138n19
Butler, Michael J., 147n19

Cadaveric organs
  causes of shortage, 20–21
  market for, contrasted with living-
    donor organs, 127–29
  markets limited to, 51
  procurement of, 9–11
  supply and demand for, 18–23,
    100–102
  See also Kidneys
Caplan, Arthur, 72, 158n18, 159n9
Cate, Fred H., 7, 49, 140nn11, 13,
  16, 17, 20, 145n3
Chapman, David E., 144n56, 147n18
Chapman, Fern Schumer, 143n52,
  145n3
Childress, James F., 70–72, 146n5
Clark, Matt, et al., 145n3
Coase, Ronald, 162n14
Cohen, Lloyd R., 144n58, 145n69,
  147n18, 149nn39, 42, 46,
  150n51, 155nn50, 51, 52, 161n5
Commercialization, 154n34

171

About the Authors

David L. Kaserman is the Torchmark Professor of Economics at Auburn University. Previously, he taught at the University of Tennessee at Knoxville and served as an economist at the U.S. Department of Housing and Urban Development, the Federal Trade Commission, and Oakridge National Laboratory. Mr. Kaserman is the author of more than 100 publications in applied microeconomics and industrial organization. His research centers on vertical integration and contractual arrangements, regulation, antitrust, telecommunications, and organ procurement policy.

A. H. Barnett is professor and chairman of the Department of Economics, International Studies, and Public Administration at the American University of Sharjah in the United Arab Emirates. Previously, he taught at Auburn University and the University of South Carolina at Columbia. His research focuses on the deregulation of public utilities, health policy, and environmental economics.

www.ingramcontent.com/pod-product-compliance
Lightning Source LLC
Jackson TN
JSHW011929131224
75386JS00034B/1117